The Poetry of the Word in Psychoanalysis

The Poetry of the Word in Psychoanalysis presents selected key papers by leading Spanish psychoanalyst Pere Folch Mateu. The pieces chosen for this book address clinical, psychopathological, technical and theoretical issues approached in Folch Mateu's unique style, providing an introduction to his impressive output. Folch Mateu integrates a wide range of psychoanalytic sources – Freud, Klein and Bion, and French psychoanalysis – in approaching topics like the psychoanalytic process, obsessive modes of control, the pathology of the negative and intellectual inhibition. The author's interest in exploring the interactions between the analyst and the patient in minute detail through the course of the psychoanalytic process is a key theme that emerges throughout, as is his devotion to the intersections between music, literature and psychoanalysis. *The Poetry of the Word in Psychoanalysis* will be of great interest to psychoanalysts and psychotherapists in practice and in training, particularly those wishing to explore the boundaries of psychoanalysis and the integration of different psychoanalytic approaches.

Pere Folch Mateu (1919–2013) co-founded the Spanish Psychoanalytic Society in 1959, teaching and influencing generations of psychoanalysts. During his long professional life he was a leader in his field, continuously updating his thought and clinical work.

J. O. Esteve is a senior member of the Spanish Psychoanalytical Society. He has applied psychoanalysis to all levels of interaction and human development, from infancy to adulthood and old age, in individual, group and institutional settings, always inspired by the teachings of Pere Folch. He is the president of the Editorial Board of the Association Monografies de Psicoteràpia, Psicoanàlisi i Salut Mental.

Jordi Sala is a clinical psychologist, training analyst of the Spanish Psychoanalytical Society, General Editor of the EPF (2004–2008) as well as of the *Catalan Review of Psychoanalysis* (2004–2013), editor of the book *Focal Psychotherapy in Children*, member of the Editorial Board of the Association Monografies de Psicoteràpia, Psicoanàlisi i Salut Mental (MPPSM). He works in private practice and in public mental health with children, adolescents and adults.

The International Psychoanalytical Association Psychoanalytic Ideas and Applications Series

Series Editor: Silvia Flechner

Femininity, Desire and Sublimation in Psychoanalysis
From the Melancholic to the Erotic
Elda Abrevaya

What Nazism Did to Psychoanalysis
Laurence Kahn

The Deconstruction of Narcissism and the Function of the Object
Explorations in Psychoanalysis
René Roussillon

The Infinite Infantile and the Psychoanalytic Task
Psychoanalysis with Children, Adolescents and their Families
Edited by Nilde Parada Franch, Christine Anzieu-Premmereur, Mónica Cardenal and Majlis Winberg Salomonsson

A Psychoanalytic Understanding of Trauma
Post-Traumatic Mental Functioning, the Zero Process, and the Construction of Reality
Joseph Fernando

The Poetry of the Word in Psychoanalysis
Selected Papers of Pere Folch Mateu
Edited by J.O. Esteve and Jordi Sala

The Freudian Matrix of André Green
Towards a Psychoanalysis for the 21st Century
Edited by Howard B. Levine

Desire, Pain and Thought
Primal Masochism and Psychoanalytic Theory
Marilia Aisenstein

The Poetry of the Word in Psychoanalysis

Selected Papers of Pere Folch Mateu

Edited by J. O. Esteve and Jordi Sala

Translated from Catalan to English by Roger Marshall and Julie Wark

Under the linguistic supervision of Christine English

Routledge
Taylor & Francis Group

LONDON AND NEW YORK

Cover image: Portrait of Pere Folch Mateu, by Elena Fieschi.

First published
by Routledge
605 Third Avenue, New York, NY 10158

and by Routledge
4 Park Square, Milton Park, Abingdon, Oxon OX14 4RN

Routledge is an imprint of the Taylor & Francis Group, an informa business

First English edition published 2023

First Catalan edition published by Monografies de Psicoteràpia, Psicoanàlisi i Salut Mental 2021

Translated from Catalan to English by Roger Marshall and Julie Wark, under the linguistic supervision of Christine English.

Library of Congress Cataloging-in-Publication Data
Names: Mateu, Pere Folch, 1919-2013 author. | Esteve, J. O., editor. | Sala, Jordi (Clinical psychologist), editor.
Title: The poetry of the word in psychoanalysis : selected papers of Pere Folch Mateu / Pere Folch Mateu ; [edited by] J. O. Esteve, Jordi Sala.
Other titles: Poesia de la paraula en psicoanàlisi. English
Description: Abingdon, Oxon ; New York, NY : Routledge, 2023. |
Series: The international psychoanalytical association psychoanalytic ideas and applications series | "Translated from Catalan to English by Roger Marshall and Julie Wark Under the linguistic supervision of Christine English"--Title page. | Includes bibliographical references and index. |
Identifiers: LCCN 2022041908 (print) | LCCN 2022041909 (ebook) | ISBN 9781032378961 (hbk) | ISBN 9781032378954 (pbk) | ISBN 9781003342472 (ebk)
Subjects: LCSH: Psychoanalysis. | Mateu, Pere Folch, 1919-2013.
Classification: LCC BF173 .M356855 2023 (print) | LCC BF173 (ebook) |
DDC 150.19/5--dc23/eng/20221017
LC record available at https://lccn.loc.gov/2022041908
LC ebook record available at https://lccn.loc.gov/2022041909

ISBN: 978-1-032-37896-1 (hbk)
ISBN: 978-1-032-37895-4 (pbk)
ISBN: 978-1-003-34247-2 (ebk)

DOI: 10.4324/9781003342472

Typeset in Palatino
by Taylor & Francis Books

This book has received support from The Melanie Klein
Trust

Contents

Note from the Editors

It has been an enormous pleasure to be involved in the process of editing this book. This is a debt that we owed to the author, from whom we have received priceless psychoanalytical teaching, and many lessons in humanity. The book consists of ten selected papers by Pere Folch Mateu (1919–2013), a well-known training analyst and author in the fields of psychoanalysis and mental health in Catalonia and Spain. But the author is little known among English speaking psychoanalysts. In his teaching and his work he is remarkable for his originality in successfully and coherently blending different psychoanalytical sources: Freudian, French psychoanalysis, Kleinian and Bionian thought. He devoted endless efforts to promoting psychoanalysis, and encouraging mental health professionals to undergo psychoanalytical training. In his aim of spreading psychoanalysis, he supported the translation of the most outstanding psychoanalytical works, inspiring and founding a psychoanalytic editorial initiative in Catalan, as well as a Journal, both still active. In the same spirit he founded and taught in institutions devoted to the promotion of individual and group psychoanalytical psychotherapy in public mental health, at a time when attention to the mental health of the general public was conspicuous by its absence. His life was that of an authentic pioneer in many respects.

The works selected for this book include clinical, psychopathological, technical and theoretical issues treated in the author's unique style, and exemplifying his extensive output. His interest in the analyst's mental activity, which permeates his entire opus, is reflected in the way he explores, in the minutest detail, the interactions between the analyst and the patient during the course of the psychoanalytic process. The topics range from technical approaches to intellectual inhibition, obsessive modes of control, pathology of the negative and others – in which he draws attention to several technical difficulties in the interpretative work – to papers devoted to the work of interpretation, containment, acting and symbol formation, specifically in the musical and literary processes. In the case of the latter, he offers us an original approach to the intersection between these creative fields with psychoanalytic work.

Pere Folch Mateu was endowed with a profound poetic and artistic sensibility, which he put at the service of clinical, technical, and theoretical psychoanalysis, and to the teaching of it. He had a passionate love for all manifestations of language, its richness and its communicative possibilities. That is why we as editors, as well as our colleagues in Monografies de Psicoteràpia, Psicoanàlisi i Salut Mental, agreed that this collection of his works should be titled *The Poetry of the Word in Psychoanalysis*.

We are certain that the book will be of great interest to those psychoanalysts and psychotherapists who wish to explore how theory and technique can benefit from a creative integration of different psychoanalytic sources, as seen in the works of an inspired and original author.

We would like to express our gratitude to Michael Feldman, Robert Caper and John Steiner for their support and to our colleagues in the MPPSM Association, Lluís Albaigés, Enric Canyadell, Esperança Castell, Elena Fieschi, Antònia Grimalt, Francesc Pareja, Anna Romagosa and Mabel Silva, without whose efforts and contributions this book would not have been possible. And last, but not least, we would like to express thanks to Silvia Flechner, Chair of the IPA Publications Committee, who took on this project enthusiastically making the publication possible.

J. O. Esteve and Jordi Sala, editors

Foreword

The Publications Committee of the International Psychoanalytic Association is pleased to present a new volume of the International Psychoanalysis Library series.

It is a great honor as new Chair of the Publications Committee of the International Psychoanalytic Association to continue the long journey founded in 1991 by Robert Wallerstein and most recently continued by Gabriela Legorreta to continue the tradition of selected books.

We present the book *The Poetry of the Word in Psychoanalysis*, written by Pere Folch Mateu. He was Training Analyst of the Spanish Psychoanalytical Society (International Psychoanalytic Association), creator of the *Revista Catalana de Psicoanalisi* and of the New Collection of Psychoanalysis and Psychotherapy Monographs. He taught at the Central University of Barcelona and the Université of Paris 7.

His papers were selected by Jordi Sala and J. O. Esteve. It is a tribute to the enormous body of work that has left his mark on all those who had the opportunity to come in contact with Pere Folch.

I want to thank Jordi Sala for illuminating me about the life and thought of this author through a lengthy interview conducted with Pere Folch in 2011.

We generally have an understanding of various psychoanalytic authors without necessarily knowing their personal life. In this case especially, I considered it necessary to provide some points from this long interview because Pere Folch's life story is inextricably tied to the practice of his profession as a psychoanalyst.

In the interview he recounts different moments of his life, including memories of his childhood that left deep marks on his personality.

He was born in Barcelona. With the death of his maternal grandparents, the family was reduced to himself, his parents and a sister a few years older. The sudden death of his sister at the age of 22 due to polio (Landry Syndrome) was a cruel, catastrophic experience when Pere Folch was around 16–17 years old. Until that point everything had been relatively easy and full of hope, despite a modest economic situation.

He was the son of parents who were simple but full of social and cultural ideals. They wanted their children to reach the cultural-societal level they had not been able themselves to achieve. Pere found this enthusiasm of his parents extraordinary. However, everything was interrupted by the death of his sister at the beginning of 1936, as well as the start of the civil war.

His mother tongue and his culture were Catalan. However, he spoke Spanish perfectly. This bilingualism led him to intuitive thinking about semantic correspondences and etymological questions which go unnoticed by the monolingual.

He was known for his enjoyment of literature and poetry, leading him to value and appreciate the potentiality of language. In his adolescence, in Barcelona, French culture had an extensive influence. Pere Folch lived in Paris before having been in Madrid. He remembered Ortega y Gasset's continual reference to German philosophers and essayists. This prompted him to study German. Heine and Rilke had begun to be published in a bilingual version, and from this followed his interest in Freud and the value of the German language.

He later learned English to keep up with British psychoanalytic literature, mainly stimulated by years of analysis in London with Dr Donald Meltzer amongst other analysts.

Before studying English, he learned what he considered the most challenging and beloved language – Finnish – his wife's mother tongue – a language with a strange and complex structure for a Latin speaker.

His interest in psychoanalysis was linked mainly to his adolescent experiences: sexuality, disillusionment with childhood religiosity, the tragic experience of his sister's death, but also death anxieties later reactivated by the civil war, while in the social plane, mourning and so many illusions that were proscribed by the dictatorship.

His stay in Paris was his first contact with a psychoanalytic society. He attended an outreach course organized by the Paris Psychoanalytic Society, given by essential and famous psychoanalysts.

Along with Pere Bofill and Julia Coromines, who followed the guidelines for proper training in the 1950s, he followed training in France, Switzerland, and London. Dr. René Diatkine traveled to Barcelona for supervision and seminars. According to Pere Folch, the excellent relationship with the Paris Society, favoured by Diatkine and by Pierre Marty, facilitated recognition as a Study Group and later as a Society recognized by the International Psychoanalytic Association.

His stay in London led him to meet D. W. Winnicott, then President of the British Society. His supervisors were Kleinian. As a complement to his training, he supervised with Dr. H. Rosenfeld, E. Bick, and H. Segal, starting first with her in child psychoanalysis and later followed with Betty Joseph.

In his paper *Literary Process and Psychoanalytical Process* (April 1990), Folch describes "Analogies and Contrasts" between two different types of interpersonal relationships: on the one hand, the relationship between the psychoanalyst and their patient and, on the other, the relationship between the author and the reader.

His papers demonstrate the influence of literary works by which he was nourished, as well as his experience as a psychoanalyst, allowing him to consider "Transference as a phenomenon that is common and central both to the analytical situation and to the literary one": which as he says, is indispensable for initiating a process of change in either the patient or the reader.

For Folch, the phenomenon of transference can be found in various settings, and he explains that "Freud chose the polysemic term *Übertragung* to denote such a generic phenomenon, a term which, in modern German, means to transport, translate or contaminate, or to transfer money ... By situating this concept at the core of the analytical situation, this transport, traffic, can be made to apply to all kinds of psychic activities: the transposition or transference of impulses, feelings, images, and intimate unconscious situations".

We are grateful to Jordi Sala and his colleagues, for bringing together an excellent selection of Pere Folch's work. This new book will be of great value and a legacy of these psychoanalysts who wish to present their knowledge of an author with a particular sensibility and inspiration.

I also want to thank Gabriela Legorreta – past Chair and Advisor of our Committee – for the generous help she gave me throughout my work for this project. I also want to express my gratitude to Rhoda Bawdekar, Web and Publications Manager, for her unconditional assistance.

Silvia Flechner
Series Editor
Chair, IPA Publications Committee

Introduction

This book represents but a small sample of Pere Folch's thinking based on his long experience as a clinician, researcher, teacher, and supervisor, concerning the nature of understanding, the psychoanalytic process, and changes of perspective in the process of research and theoretical developments. Everyone who knew him can bear witness to his vitality, his dry sense of humour, the incisiveness of his thinking together with a deep respect for people's ideas. He was never directly critical of anyone's work and was always eager to offer another point of view without discounting what they had to say.

Pere Folch's interest in the analyst's mental processes led him to explore in the minutest detail the interactions with the patient. I would like to draw particular attention to his emphasis on the experiential and the interactive, at a time when the prevailing approach focused mainly on the patient's intra-psychic conflicts, which is fully illustrated with the generosity of his clinical explorations.

This spirit of research is reflected in the exploration of learning difficulties in two clinical cases, with a minute descriptive observation of the vicissitudes of the interaction. The interpretations of attacks on linking and the patient's attack on his own perceptive and cognitive functions were felt as a threat to his narcissistic organization. It prompted the hypothesis of projection of primary mental activities such as memory, attention, and judgement into the analyst, to safeguard these capacities. This resulted in a more effective approach. In this way the author introduces us to the importance of micro-communications in the session. In this first paper (Chapter 1), Folch's aim is to explore the scope and limitations of the concept of *inhibition of psychic functions*, which he describes from a binocular perspective: a parallel consideration of the level and quality of the function, on the one hand, and the state of the object relation on the other. In keeping with the line taken by Bion in his synopsis of the states of development of thought (the Grid), Folch suggests a genetic criterion as an organizing principle for a classification of psychic functions.

Chapter 2, which contains lexically rich descriptions of his systematic observations of newborn babies and numerous clinical vignettes, explores the nuances involved in the concept of control and the ways in which it impinges upon the Self in relation to the Object: from the intrapsychic situation to the interpersonal relationship, the two being interconnected by reciprocity, complementarity or consonance. It is not possible to believe in a specificity typical of a particular nosological entity. The spectrum of phantasies and actions extends to all cases, with a use which ranges from the most structuring aims to the most elemental defence mechanisms. The analyst, upon experiencing the evocative or provocative induction stimulus (sensory, ultra-sensory, or even extra-sensory) from the analysand, summons within himself those corresponding symmetrical phantasies that match the analysand's experience. The analyst runs the risk of being imprisoned within a projective counter-identification, thus becoming moralistic and trying to interpret what he sees as an "obsessive trick". The patient's intellectualizing agility, with marginalization of affects, prompts us to examine the content too closely, at the expense of gaining an understanding of the attitude or atmosphere of the session, on account of their very effective "acting out". Only the acknowledgement of our countertransference can enable us to recover our freedom of thought.

Particularly interesting, inspiring and creative is The Literary Process and The Psychoanalytical Process in Chapter 3, where Folch invites us to explore similarities and contrasts between two different types of interpersonal relationships: the psychoanalyst and the patient, and the relationship between the author (or the text) and the reader. The analytical situation occurs in a fruitful, asymmetrical exchange which favours the dramatization of the patient's deepest, most inveterate structures. The relationship between the author or text and the reader is also asymmetrical but the exchange is unidirectional. However, the relationship with the author takes place inwardly, in the reader's psychic reality, and can be extremely intense. Folch proposes looking more closely at the particularities of the communicative relationship that is established between the author and reader, with reference to the relationship between analyst and patient.

The consideration of the analyst–analysand interaction and its setting as an ideal space for the symbolization of the unconscious, understood as the dramatization, updating, and verbalization of the analysand's internal object relations is the theme of Chapter 4. Also discussed is the evolution of the quality of the symbol in parallel with the establishment, evolution, and interpretation of the transference. Fluctuations in the structure of any symbolic formation are related to oscillations between *insight* and resistance. The notion of false symbols is connected with the incessant interaction of integration and *splitting* of the symbol and diabolon, of truth and deception.

The complex interaction of love and hatred, the clinical corollary of the elemental conflict between the life and the death drives, unfolding in a variety of ways is the focus of Chapter 5. There is a gradient: "falsehoods" → lies → Lies. This is illustrated by the clinical course of certain forms of positive transference, which progress from a form of idealized exaltation of the analyst and the analytical method to a growing and painful acceptance of their limitations. The analyst faces a delicate task if they want to avoid a double pitfall: on the one hand, a collusive idealization which seeks the chronic avoidance of conflict; on the other, the over-hasty reduction of "transference love" and enthusiastic imitation to an ever-present defence mechanism. In order to avoid both pitfalls, what matters is to highlight the relationship between idealization and the patient's despair. The mimetic attitudes of the patient and the conscious, fervent imitation that characterize the first stages of treatment is a hypocritical attitude which, far from being fraudulent and renegade, consciously imitates the admired object and strives to conceal a shame-inducing past. The hypocritical behaviour in the sessions, a self-pitying and playful submission in a so-called "servitude to the analysis", for the sake of a modest approximation to the difficult truth about themselves; a truth which they recognize as desirable and dreaded at the same time.

The psychoanalyst must be able to notice the expressive richness of all the preverbal signs and symbols. It is necessary to become familiar with this primitive language: a visceral, sensorial, emotional language which hasn't yet acquired semantic precision. Chapter 6 concerns musical elements of preverbal communication and musical elements of verbal language: vital sentiments and categorical sentiments. Listening to a musical composition arouses in the listener a range of affects, feelings, memories, and fantasies that vary from subject to subject, regardless of the composer's intentions. What happens in this evocative process of listening to a musical work? The psychoanalyst tries to explain the listener's relationship with music according to the pattern of his object relations. Like any aesthetic experience, the musical work awakens a complex transferential process. Music is a particularly apt container where listeners can project their individual internal situations which are mobilized by listening.

Folch made his own personal distillation of Bion, which is reflected in his creative development, in Chapter 7, of the **binocular vision** concept as a conjugation of two vertices of the same experience. This model pertains to a clinical and technical reality, out of which the psychoanalyst forms a representation; it depends on the convergent vision of more than one point of view. He points out the connection that requires the use of binocular vision: the link between the group and the individual therapeutic experience, between the group mind and the individual mind. Considering the session as a group of two people, the author highlights the importance of the link between the gregarious-group sector and the individual sector of the personality: between *groupality* and *subjectality* that *would* be present in every individual. The nature of the personality as a whole would depend on the particular linking between each of these, whether this is a harmonious conjunction, a confusion, or an extreme disjunction between these two modes of psychic functioning.

In psychoanalysis the notion of the negative is characterized by intense ambiguity. If, on the one hand, it serves the mechanisms of various psychopathological disorders, on the other, we recognize virtue in mental functions and attitudes that are either characterized by absence or suspended. If negation, denial, and foreclosure are at the basis of the psychotic or perverse organization, we also value, in accordance with Bion, *negative capability*, considering that insight may be obtained through freeing ourselves of memory, desire, and the urgent need to understand. In this regard, negativity can be in the service of creativity, increasing our capacity for attention and presence. Like light and shadow, positivity and negativity are embedded in the flow of our experience. This mutual involvement of absence and presence are part of the dialectic of opposites that psychoanalysis has constantly highlighted. In clinical practice we find this entanglement of creativity and the pathology of the negative to which the author refers. Clinical material and technical approach guidelines are included in this Chapter 8.

Inspired by Bion's concepts of containment, transformation, and emotional experience together with the container–contained relationship and PS <—> D oscillation which have a preeminent role in the evolution of the patient–analyst relationship and in the therapeutic process. In Chapter 9 the author deploys an exhaustive exploration of these terms with an important section on technique, giving particular attention to the differences between sympathy and empathy, in relation to interpretation. The psychoanalytic con-versation as a two-person matter underlines how the process of transformation of the patient's message does not begin with an interpretation but with the patient's way of seeing and hearing the analyst.

Chapter 10 is extremely rich, complex, and original. Folch illustrates his clinical and creative research into the variations in approach while carrying out the task of analysis. He refers to two contrasting nuances in the analyst's receptive, cogitative, and expressive style. The poetic, or lyrical way of engaging would be, initially, expressed through the analyst's intimate emotional resonance with the patient: it is a state of mind in which living an experience takes precedence over understanding it. In contrast with this poetic manner of engaging, there is a tendency to organize and hierarchize. The desire to understand predominates, and it constrains the expansive development of the lived experience. The logical and the lyrical could be loosely compared with the frequently recalled sense-versus-sensibility binary. They not only denote behavioural styles but also ways of being emotionally affected: in other words, receptive styles, the two not being mutually exclusive. By paying attention to the course of the counter-transference, the analyst can become aware of the fluctuations in their receptive, cogitative and expressive style. The Logical and the Lyrical are connected with certain features of paranoid-schizoid and depressive organizations, as well as with Bion's concept of PS <-> D fluctuations.

Antònia Grimalt and Mabel Silva

1   Clinical Problems of Intellectual Inhibition[1]

Pere Folch Mateu

Clinical Problems of Intellectual Inhibition

This paper explores some of the difficulties experienced in the psychoanalytic treatment of a neurotic child and a borderline adult. Both patients' initial symptomology was characterized by serious difficulties in their school and professional performance respectively, although the request for help was not exclusively based on these problems. Both child and adult came to the therapeutic relationship with the burden of particular learning difficulties which included an incorrect use of language, extreme attention deficit and an apparent ineptness when it came to linking up aspects of their psychic experience.

The heavy load of internal and external conflicts seemed to be obscured, especially in the adult, by an impoverishment or slowing down of psychic functioning. Reiterative behaviour also lent the sessions an impassive quality, week after week. This inhibition of basic psychic functions seemed to hamper any prospect of useful work. Indeed the very intensity of the work invited repeated interpretation of attacks on linking, including of the patient's attack on his own perceptive and cognitive functions. The reaction to such interpretation was often the shoring up of the mechanism, which resulted in an even more intense deterioration of receptive possibilities.

It often seemed to me that any consideration of deficit, however much its defensive value against anxiety was clarified, caused the patient to feel alarm at the collapse of his narcissistic organization. As such, I began to highlight more positively the tacit load I felt the patient was placing upon me, with the projection of primary mental activities such as memory, attention and judgement into me, to safeguard these capacities. These were then no longer being attacked by the patient, but had been resituated for prudent working on in my mental sphere. Even so, the patient often mistrusted my mental activity, or this making of myself, as he saw it, a custodian of his memory, his capacity to discriminate between inside and outside, good and bad, and so on. Since the patient had objectivized and then situated these functions, these prerequisites of interpretation, in me,

DOI: 10.4324/9781003342472-1

various phenomena, anecdotes or circumstances he described became hazy. Interpretations were then hard to form. On other occasions however, an interpretation emerged painlessly and without too much suffering, from fairly clear material. In such cases the interpretation, and also those preceding it, could be recognized by the patient as pertaining to him.

Reviewing my notes and reflecting upon the fluctuation of my analytic function in the course of these treatments, I realize that I had begun to do without interpretations which, more or less, tried to confront the patient with the meagre yield of his defences. Interpretations I did make also took into account the significant anxiety that could be triggered in the patient, who couldn't stand much complexity and opposition of meanings. I found these could reduce the extent of the patient's cognitive inhibition and enable a better knowledge of his own, and the other's internal experience.

The borderline patient, a man of over thirty, was an engineer, married with children. He was referred by a psychiatrist whose pharmacological treatment of the patient's depression, anxiety, apathy and inability to work had, after a year, come to an impasse. Prior to this treatment, over a number of years the patient's illness had manifested in several crises from which he had only partially emerged, with somewhat diminished capacities and an increased addiction to secondary gains of a very passive nature. Some years earlier he had undergone electroconvulsive therapy and sleep cures. When he had resided abroad, he had attempted a psychoanalytic treatment but said he had ended this because he saw no results after six months. Upon his return to Barcelona, he embarked on another attempt at psychoanalysis, but after two months this became unbearable for him, and he returned to pharmacological treatment with another psychiatrist.

The patient's family situation was quite deranged. He was financially dependent on his parents, since he had made little progress in his career. His wife stayed at home managing the house and the children's education. A year before seeing me the couple had stopped having intercourse because of intense dyspareunia. When he telephoned me to request an appointment, I had the impression of a semi-drugged, confused person, who expressed himself very ponderously. The first time I saw him, his presence was discordant, as though his gaze was childish, he had a heavy air about him, was hunched over and walked with small steps, almost like an old man. His use of language was parsimonious. He used formal expressions borrowed from the psychiatric vocabulary, and spoke reservedly. He was seemingly very attentive to the consequences that a piece of information shared by him might bring as a specific therapeutic measure: an encouragement to leave his job, a suggestion to adjust the dosage of tranquilizers, recommendation of a new sleep cure, and so on. Any attempt to more fully understand his experience of the symptoms, which included headaches, intercostal neuralgia and a tendency to catch colds, was received with great suspicion. Without letting me speak, he would interrupt, saying, "I assure you, this pain is real". He was terribly suspicious that my treatment would basically consist in a condemnation of the side benefits of his illness, his verbal relationship with the psychiatrist seemingly being limited to this topic. He was most disconcerted when I talked about aspects of his life which he felt had been ravaged by his illness: his unhappy home and working life, his children whom he barely knew, his shut-down sexuality and resolute yearning to live in a vegetative state without conflict.

During the treatment, the patient's powerful sense of persecution by objects became focused entirely on the vexatious head of the department in which he worked, who treated him roughly, offensively, even brutally. Any attempt to understand, in the transference, his difficulty in being helped, or any consideration of his resentment at not being free of any stimulus or desire, was received by the patient with the sincere belief that I was confused. This prompted him to repeat exactly the same information. If I insisted, highlighting this repetition, he responded less good-naturedly, saying he had already made it clear to me that he was talking about "thingamajig" and not "thingamabob", and once again repeated his unvarying story. I understood categorically then, that I was tied to the patient's concrete thinking and that any attempt I might make to provide an analogical link with his story was a totally solitary endeavour. The patient clearly felt that I was on a wrong path, from which he had to lead me back into communing with his immutable version of things.

Recognition of the transference entails, in fact, a level of symbolic relationship that my patient hadn't achieved or, better said, which he had lost in his growing intolerance of the anxiety of life. I heeded Rosenfeld's technical recommendations at that time, and gave up the idea of pointing out any correspondence between internal and external objects, and between the therapeutic relationship and his family and professional relationships. Instead, I tried to formulate in affirmative terms any impression I had of deficit, absence, emptiness, and discontinuity. I learned to make brief interventions in simple sentences. Any subordinate or appositive clause was too much for him, and what I'd said was felt to be nothing more than a string of words. When I said something about this experience, telling him that listening to me for too long was too much for him, that it tired him, and that he wanted me close to him, he might answer, "Aren't we close? What does close mean?" And I might say, "Being with you in feeling, sharing the way we see things".

When I told him something that took him by surprise, he reacted in various strange ways. For example, shrugging, with a particular protrusion of the upper lip pushed out by the tongue from inside the mouth, and with wide-open but placid eyes, he would say, "I don't understand anything." On other occasions, he would respond with a series of jerky head-shaking movements, with violent blinking and frowning. This jumpy response, which implied some degree of reception of what I'd said, made it possible to speak of his problematic intolerance of novelty, uncertainty, strangeness, or any disagreeable feeling. When my words were able to hint at his mental disquietude, they were rapidly reduced, literally, to a specific concrete object, a fly in his ear that he had to shake out. Yet it was even more difficult to hear him respond to my interpretations with his verbal, quasi-mannerisms like, "We need to talk about that", "That's unconscious", and "I feel bad that you take it like that". Some reactions of this type were inevitably followed by others in the following terms, "Yes, you're totally right about that". It was helpful to show him that he said I was right as a matter of urgency, since he felt the frenzied need to declare that he was at one with me, or because he sensed that my ability to tolerate his systematic rejection was foundering.

My patient was bitterly affronted by any intervention I made that was not in keeping with his demands. These might include that I telephone his psychiatrist to arrange a new sleep cure, that I agree he ought to be pre-scribed new tranquilizers, or that I prepare a statement justifying a few days of sick leave which might be presented to the company where he worked. One dramatic action followed upon another. For example, the patient once arrived with his wife so that she could see *in situ* what an insensitive doctor he had to deal with. He would telephone his psychiatrist to inform him of his more frequently recurring ideas of suicide, and would be uncooperative in sessions in which he accused me of refusing to prevent disasters, either for him or his family because he said he didn't feel able to stop torturing them. In all these extreme situations, what was most arduous was that even the simplest and most cautious invitation from me to approach the problem from a dif-ferent direction was stripped by the patient of any meaning. Such an invitation, since it was neither a yes nor a no to his demands, was entirely unwelcome. Any intervention I made was responded to with insistent questions such as, "What am I supposed to do?", and "Don't you see that I can't go out?"

It was around that time that the patient gave me a concrete illustration of how helpless he felt. It was a very rainy day and he came to his session soaked from head to foot. His hair was sopping and messily plastered all over his cheeks. His raincoat dripped everywhere, and he carried a folder which had also been damaged by the drenching. I found him standing in the waiting room with papers in hand and his raincoat still buttoned up. When I greeted him, he answered with a simple, "Look", indicating his physical state. I recalled his early insistence that he couldn't go out. Then, I would have pointed out to him his need for concrete help, and this was an effective response to his constant wondering about what he was sup-posed to do. Now, I commented that his need for me, which he expressed on this wretched wet day was directly conveyed, unlike in sessions that began with him going to the toilet. Today, he was demanding that I myself and not my cloakroom had to take charge of all this wetness and also his tears. He stopped me, saying that what was happening was that it was raining a lot. Once I'd taken in this retort, I thought that the patient was attempting to restrict my thinking about anything other than what was most obvious. In arriving so wet through, he was teaching me that only tangible illustrations would be of any use in this treatment. I think that I was able to get through to him in a series of interventions that helped him understand the way in which he expressed or evacuated his needs. For example, in bringing the rain into my home that day, my patient unquestionably made internal something that was external. Noting this, I could help my patient see something more of what was inside himself, simply by inviting him to look.

However, any greater receptivity he was able to tolerate after that day was undermined over and over again with his alarmed protests about the excessive mental activity work that I submitted him to. He would also respond with obsessive rumination. He could say very straightforwardly, following the second or third intervention of the session, "Don't you see that if you say so many things, I'll end up crazy?" Sometimes his reaction to the overload of a session in which he had managed to be more attentive was less direct. For example, he came one day not complaining that I made him think too much, but explaining that he couldn't stop thinking about whether or not he'd left a distilling device properly secured. It was the end of the week and he feared that he might find it broken on Monday. He had already checked the device because he'd gone back to the laboratory four times with different excuses, but he didn't know if he should go again after finishing the session with me. He'd have to come up with a new excuse so the caretaker wouldn't be surprised by so many comings and goings. In a new approximation to the transference, I told him that he was contrasting my way of calmly leaving him on Friday evening with his protective, edgy, finicky way of taking his leave from his work, and from the fragile apparatus that could come loose, become unscrewed, or fall apart. This linked up with the vicissitudes of weekend life at home and his feeling that I was unable to appreciate the trials and tribulations he would have to endure before returning to see me on Monday. Then, I noted that it was more possible for him to consider the transference relationship with me when it was illustrated through his treatment of things, than it was through connecting his interpersonal anecdotes to our relationship.

One step forward, although it was painful, came when my patient began to feel sorrow upon recognizing that he was rancorous. Such rancour he experienced as feeling clingy towards people like his wife and his parents. This was quite different from what he'd said some time earlier, which was that when driven by vexation, he would torture the people closest to him. Rather, his sorrow came not at a time of unmanageable impulsion but when there was more contact with the image of another who could recognize the abusive tone of his recriminatory complaints. It coincided with the ability to remember a few dreams, and even to accept some act of kindness from his head of department, whom my patient had previously found so vexing. However, everything could be spoilt if, going further with an interpretation, I connected his excessive rancour on feeling badly treated by this person or that, with his experience of being with a Prussian analyst, as he put it, who was now being perceived as perhaps less stern. His fear of the immediate demands that this recognition would make on him was such that he could suddenly return to a tetchy refusal to consider any aspect of his inner world, grumbling that I was pushing him into intolerable tasks. "Leave me alone. My head's spinning", he said one regressive day, referring to concerns of the moment. I told him that I saw progress in his ability to be concerned about the day's different challenges and things he had to manage. I evaluated as positive the comparison he made between his boss, and his mind which had a good measure of ability. This enraged him and he said that by supporting such tenuous signs of progress, I was oblivious to the fact that he couldn't take any more, that his head felt like a drum. I was then able to interpret the violence with which he'd rid himself of his developing containing capacity, of his mind that was newly populated with concerns, in order to have this empty drum head in which my words could only be a painful racket.

Incidents like this were followed by somatizations, insistent consultations with his psychiatrist, and criticism of my technique in terms similar to those he used when speaking about his boss after he'd been chastised for some badly done job. Interpreting both this connection and his identification with this Prussian superior who found fault with his technical clumsiness had little resonance right then. He repeated that he couldn't follow his boss's explanations and returned to badmouthing him.

I would like to reiterate here, that my transference interpretations were sometimes more acceptable and could be better understood by the patient when his material dealt with impersonal objects. I shall give one final example. For some days he had been complaining that people didn't pay attention to him, and that it was evident that when he was well treated, he was capable of good performance. One evening he was very irate when he came because after having spent five or six hours monitoring the course of a laboratory reaction, he had still been criticized for not being diligent enough. He told me in great detail about the difficulties of dealing with potassium dichromate and of keeping it liquid; that if you get distracted for even the tiniest moment it crystallizes and the reaction has to be started all over again, that it needs a precise optimum temperature, that there are difficulties with adding water, and so on. Here, I could speak to him of the technique that he wanted to inspire in me, in which I would never lapse in my continuous, uninterrupted attention. I also told him that he recognized the difficulty of dealing with this baby part of him, a baby that in the laboratory was called potassium dichromate, and which in the sessions could be disturbed by too few or too many explanations, or by too much or too little vehemence. Then, all fluidity was lost and we had to go back to square one.

I shall now give some very fragmentary information about the case of the small boy I referred to at the beginning of this paper. I would like to focus specifically on the inhibitory aspect of the symptoms that led to his treatment, which were expressed vividly in the transference. The boy was seven and a half when he began treatment, and in addition to character difficulties (jealous rivalry with his siblings, episodic bulimia, indifference to warnings or inability to heed them, cold indifference when punished, and persistence with catastrophic behaviour patterns, et cetera), his performance at school had deteriorated in the last year. For example, he had made no progress in arithmetic, but repeated capricious errors of the same kind; he was very slow at reading, exhibited variable dysorthography, and wrote illegibly. However, what was really disturbing was his motor instability and such a degree of attention deficit that he stubbornly resisted any material he was given in the hope that it might interest him. Indifferent to reasoning, he objected with arguments that were surprising for a boy of his age, despite being thought to be quite smart outside of school. For example, when his father told him he had to prepare to be able to work when he was grown up, he said, apparently seriously, that there was no need since he was going to get married every day, so would get a lot of presents and would become rich. He could recall some traumatic situations related to several operations for a squint when he was twenty-two months old, and to his relationship with a psychotic brother.

From the earliest sessions, the boy developed an intense transference, much like a younger child with few defences might. At the very beginning of treatment, he expressed fears of being mistaken for his psychotic brother (who had been in treatment with my wife) and, at the same time, was worried that I wouldn't recognize him unless I thought of him in relation to his brother. This confusion of identities and of the breast-penis object, increased by the fact that his brother had been treated in my home, found the most nuanced expression in his early games with plasticine: pieces of wood were hidden in the middle of the mass of plasticine and later had to be rediscovered and distinguished from the mass, castles accommodated different pieces of wood, and, finally, a castle contained just one piece of wood inside it. Problems of division and separation were expressed, at times, in purely mathematical terms. Then, my patient would require me to be a teacher who would show him how to divide, and would ask if I knew where the piece of wood hidden in the middle of the plasticine was, how many pieces of wood there were, and if the drawers of the other children I might be treating were all the same, et cetera.

The boy showed considerable mimetic ability, surprising acceptance and deft application of my interpretations. He also displayed some seductive behaviour towards me, quite usual in his outside conduct and, in the treatment, his behaviour was intensely driven by the need for massive projective identification. It was striking to note his shrewdness of attention, mental agility, and exaltation of perceptive functions during these early months. He also made a plea, almost directly formulated, that I shouldn't disturb his illusion of an equating of identities. For example, if he'd drawn his father falling down a mountain with his skis on, and I linked that with his feeling that his relationship with his father-analyst had, during the weekend, like a breast, hill, or castle, gone wrong or been damaged, he quickly drew me another much lower mountain with his father gliding placidly down it. That could then be followed by the fast construction of a plasticine castle, very well protected, on one corner of the table with the single piece of wood inside it. It was then easy to interpret for him the prize he expected for his diligence in annulling the accident, and his anxiety lest his good relationship with me, free and devoid of tensions, wasn't quickly re-established. The seduction was also accomplished with shows of a more candid dependence, like representing himself in drawings as a little chick walking on four legs which were comparable with the four sessions which, in effect, seemed to have got him moving where previously he had been stationary, especially at school.

Interpretation of such seductions, together with the experience of the first long holiday break, mitigated his confusion about and intolerance of feeling separate from me. Recognition of situations in which he had denied such feelings didn't happen without grievance and were almost instantaneously compensated for with masturbatory activity or sexual games with his psychotic brother. This was expressed more or less directly in drawings and play, which often consisted in games in which he experienced himself as a magician. The equation of parts of himself and of the object was evident in the repertoire of tricks that he performed for me in a pantomime-like show in the sessions. His introduction of measures of obsessive control when he felt exiled, as a result of my interpretations, from his use of projective identification, was very striking.

In his drawings and his play with plasticine, there appeared different versions of the combined parent-figure. In the first session of one week, he very precisely drew a couple, both of whom were working each at his or her own task. This representation I interpreted as mitigating the unease awakened by his sense of a sexual couple, which had prompted his masturbatory activity. The patient's excessive control was also expressed in rigorous criticism of any verbal slip I made (the treatment was conducted in French) which, for him, invalidated the interpretation. His use of the toilet was also accentuated, as was his scrutiny of tiny changes in the room where he was seen, and of the household comings and goings. However, when his anxiety intensified, this control wasn't very effective, and he resorted to more magical strategies. For example, he would spend the sessions making banknotes of mounting value, or representing on paper different sports, such as football and basketball. Or, using coins, he would simulate a match in which he was invariably the winner. He would drop vowels, and use anagrams and secret codes to obscure his speech, and this made interpretation more difficult. I was however able to interpret this tenacious competition with me as concealing resentment over his failed seduction of the breast and his disappointment over the fact that it was no longer his exclusive haven and possession. I also connected this rivalry with a fear of losing everything in a countercoup in which I could strip him of all the gains made in the analysis, which were experienced by him as a furtive acquisition. He continued with more or less crude variations of his competitiveness, and was very sensitive to incidents that occurred at school, at home, or in the sessions themselves, in which he was in competition with others. He spent many days making a list of the children in his class and giving marks to each for the different subjects. He always gave himself the highest marks and got very irritated by interpretations of this manic inversion of the reality at his school, where he was among those scoring the lowest marks. Similarly in the sessions, he was often unable to learn very much from me, especially since he often wanted, by hook or by crook, to be the teacher in this setting. The external situation, however, kept improving and his performance at school in the second year of treatment improved considerably. He acquired skills in maths, automatic reading, and in his ability to pay attention.

However, at the end of the third year of treatment a very negative attitude appeared when the rivalry of some months earlier re-emerged and fully confronted him with his intense jealousy. This followed some threatening linking of partial internal objects (breast and nipple), and disappointing attempts at controlled projection into each one. This internal situation was activated by my absences from Barcelona, which he found out about by more or less indirectly asking his family. The situation of internal and transferential jealousy was acted out a lot, and was strongly connected to his psychotic brother who had started improving more and more at school and in his relationship with his parents. All of this led to long periods when my patient's attitude was arrogant in the sessions, which were now filled with incessant activity. Such activity abolished all verbal communication, including when I attempted to initiate it with my interventions. On some days, my patient spent the whole session reading books or children's magazines. On other days, play consisted in an equally prolonged game of bouncing a ball off the wall and catching it by turns with right and left hands. Or, my patient would spend the whole session with the same invariability, letting a parachutist doll fall from different heights. He could spend session after session with these indefinitely reiterated activities and was influenced neither by my interpretations nor by my silence.

I had the growing feeling that he was very resentful, even rancorous about the loss of his old defences of seduction and omnipotent fusion, denial of the precariousness of his reality at school, and his resorts to magic to maintain an omniscience in the service of control. The collapse of this defensive system, which had on the one hand brought evident progress, especially in terms of learning ability, had on the other hand tipped him into suffering. He was having to face the discrediting of his strategies, and to endure emotions like jealousy and the evident need to learn, which had previously been vehemently ruled out. In addition to the external factors to which I have referred, there was another factor that was decisive in his deterioration in the treatment. The family had decided to leave Barcelona after a year. The plan for a change of residence had been vaguely initiated on several occasions, but now the move seemed more definite. The patient hid this from me for some months, although I'd referred to it in interpreting to him his feelings about separation, identity, and distance.

Our relationship became fairly strained when I was able to use information from the family about the planned move to refer in my interpretations to fears of separation. This was in some sense humiliating for him, and made him actively and contemptuously take a distance from me. This shift on his part consisted in the denial of a process of distancing between him and his internal and external objects, and with it the denial of a progressively painful evaporation of the confusion and omnipotence. All our work until the end was an attempt to develop a less rancorous acceptance of this prolonged and brittle farewell to defensive patterns which, so idealized in other times, had been expressed in such elementary ways. No headway was made in his accepting of depressive anxieties. I believe, however, that the patient's obsessive organization became somewhat more realistic, and that improvements in terms of academic and behavioural performance were also maintained.

However, my intention in writing this paper was not so much to evaluate the evolution and outcome of this treatment, but to emphasize the features of this last, critical stage. My interpretive activity at that time was undermined by the impact on me of the patient's way of speaking and acting. Expressive though this might have been, I was overwhelmed by its poverty and restriction of content, and by everything it covered up and denied, both of in terms of my own knowledge and of the patient's internal experience.

My interpretation of his attitude aimed too much at the aggressive component of it, and had the effect of deteriorating the link between us. Further, I realize I had become less able to illustrate his anxiety. This, the patient then managed to disguise even more, both for himself and for me. Anxiety was more and more distantly inferred with this patient, and it became increasingly fleeting and hard to grasp in the present.

Close observation led me to interpretations that he experienced as controlling, such as those which referred to the alarm he felt when I referred to his negativism, which I thought was betrayed by furtive, penetrating glances from behind his book. I also interpreted the many meanings of his reading in the sessions; as distancing that was somewhere between fearful and hostile; as the manic construction of an impenetrable domain (a more realistic vestige of the old castle, or womb that I had made him abandon); as offended recognition that he had overcome his reading difficulties, and so on. I used the game with the ball as an opportunity to interpret, for example when the ball landed in my lap or came too close to my glasses. I told him that only in this way, in the form of a ball and so fast, could he get to me by way of different feelings: seeking refuge in my lap, attacking my sight so as to make me as blind as he was, in a passionate expression disguised by sullen distancing.

I often realized that I was walking a tightrope, and that his intense and limited attitude had placed me there. I felt I was working against the inhibition of so many other receptive and expressive possibilities. As with my patient's defensive reduction of thought and obsessive rituals, his attentive reading throughout the session, or his simple, dogged play seemed to drain away the possibility of any other mental activity. In the sessions, as he had previously done at school, the patient turned to the powerful inhibitory defence that was decisive in paralysing any process of insight, just as it had previously been decisive in blocking the most elementary learning.

My countertransferential experience in this long, critical stage swung erratically between feeling hampered in my own thought, which concentrically revolved around the child's stunted, stubborn acting in, through to a quite different state in which I felt my mind had been invaded by excessive suggestions. This state seemed to correspond to a forced projection of obscure dynamics, whereas my hampered thinking seemed to follow from the boy's implacable behaviour which was casting out all of my mental activity. There were also moments of irritation when his attitude, far from being absorbed and concentrated, became more apathetic, bratty, and uncooperative.

Final Comments

Description of these two cases leads to some consideration of the particular clinical difficulties raised by intellectual inhibition, or, more generally, by the inhibition of mental functions. Comparison of the two may be helpful as one tries to understand the therapeutic situation, the very meaning of the symptom and its motivations. I have aimed to offer specific instances of the interpretive stance as a way of comparing experiences, which may be especially helpful to analysts working with children or with psychotic or borderline cases with more or less recalcitrant episodes marked by inhibition. I also hope to have conveyed the countertransferential reactions that these clinical situations provoked in me and which, recalling the experience of supervisions, I saw were shared by some of my colleagues.

I think that the two cases I have presented correspond to two quite distinct types of inhibition. The first is brought about predominantly by the inhibition of very rudimentary psychic functions: the capacity to perceive external and internal reality, to pay attention, and make analogical and symbolic links. The nature of inhibition in the second case is of quite a contrasting nature. Here, it seems there is a polarization of mental activity into highly idealized partial objects. Such a polarization leads to a serious inhibition of learning. This is more akin to what Freud describes in obsessive patients, while the type of inhibition of the first, borderline patient is closer to what is usually found with the hysterical personality.

The aim of this text, apart from discussing clinical situations marked by a more or less episodic predominance of *intellectual inhibition,* has been to revise the scope and limitations of this concept or, more generally, of *inhibition of psychic functions.* The very fact of its universality (is it possible to speak of psychopathological, neurotic, or psychotic productions without reference to an inhibitory aspect?) might suggest we should leave this concept aside, or at least take note of the unhelpful way in which it could weave itself in to our descriptions of cases or into the content of our interpretations, as if this is all psychoanalytic therapy involves. Of course, all psychoanalytic therapy does, as it runs its course, modify inhibition of functions and, perhaps especially, the function of perceiving psychic reality. Thus, the history of any therapeutic process can be profiled as the laborious recovery or acquisition of functions.

However, considering inhibition of functions as both an ever-present phenomenon and at other times as a syndrome doesn't take account of either economic or structural factors. In the early pages of *Inhibitions, Symptoms and Anxiety,* Freud considers the inhibition of ego functions from one or the other perspective. For example, he sees inhibition both as resulting from the considerable expenditure of energy which impoverishes functional opportunities, and he links it to the various ways the ego has of dealing with or avoiding conflicts with the id and the superego.

Also varying in Freud are the criteria for distinguishing inhibition and symptom. Inhibition, always linked with a function, does not entail a major modification of a function, but rather a simple diminishment. When an inhibition is maintained in a purely dynamic sense, Freud inscribes it in the ego and differentiates it from the symptom, which would become constituted by the transactional confluence of id and ego.

It is on the basis of full recognition of the relational value of any function by Melanie Klein and her followers, and of the parallels between the qualities of the function and the quality of the object relation, that an inhibition of functions is now typically understood. That is, an inhibition of function may be observed in the accentuation of any pathological process or, in a regression which necessarily entails the reduction or non-development of a function. In transferential terms, I would emphasize more what takes place between analyst and patient (or between patient and external object) than what does not take place, or that is avoided, or what might have been. It should be noted, though, that an interpretation generally attending to anxiety and the defence against it, frequently refers to the dispossession of functional possibilities that impoverish, distort or pervert, et cetera, the object relation.

Continuing with this parallel consideration of the level and quality of the function, on the one hand, and the state of the object relation on the other, a genetic criterion could be used as an organizing principle for a classification of psychic functions. This is the line taken by Bion in his (the grid) synopsis of the states of development of thought.

A broader and more detailed hierarchy of functions could be represented in a pyramid form, with the simplest, most elemental functions at the base, as the prerequisites of other more complex types. The most differentiated functions would appear at the apex of the pyramid. Such a representation would have to take into account particular functional achievements, mental activities in the sense that Bion described in *Elements of Psychoanalysis*, which are constitutive of more complex functions, but that are in themselves insufficient to constitute a function.

Also important would be the study of the univectorial development of functions of defensive or compensatory value. These would naturally influence, and may conform with or diverge from, the relation of the self and the internal object and external object respectively (see Freud in "Fetishism", a study of defence mechanisms in fetishism, and "Formulations on the Two Principles of Mental Functioning").

Note

1 1975, unpublished.

Bibliography

Bion, W. R. (1963/1984) *Elements of Psychoanalysis*, Karnac, London.
Bion, W. R. (1977/1989) *Two Papers: The Grid and the Caesura*, Karnac, London.
Freud, S. (1911) Formulations on the two principles of mental functioning, in *The Standard Edition of the Complete Psychological Works of Sigmund Freud, Volume* XII.
Freud, S. (1926) Inhibitions, symptoms and anxiety, in *The Standard Edition of the Complete Psychological Works of Sigmund Freud, Volume* XX.

2 Control of the Self and of the Object According to the Obsessive Relational Model[1]

Pere Folch Mateu

Control of the Self and of the Object according to the Obsessive Relational Model

The term "control" has quite precise and also nuanced connotations: vigilance, sustained attention, painstaking verification and, at a transitive level, the guiding and restricting of people and things. In French dictionaries, and in those of other languages in which "control" is referred to as a Gallicism, the polysemic definitions of the word always associate it on the one hand with inspection, checking and verification, and on the other with censure, criticism, command, and active coercion. We also realize that the notion of control includes, in psychoanalysis, its application to the object, and to oneself.

Freud (1905, 1913, 1937) used the concept in different senses, and in terms which reflect two main streams also signalled by linguists: the control of one's own drives, and the control of the object. Indeed, *Triebsbeherrschung* (literally mastery over the drive) – and *Bemächtigungstrieb* (the drive to possess, or to acquire power) express the two extremes of application of the drive, whose tendency is to control the self and the object.

While etymologically speaking, "control", which derives from "contrerôle", is close in meaning to the notion of defence, or of counterinvestment, when referring to the control of an object, the word is associated rather with the drive, which animates the desire to possess or exert power over the object.

I shall be considering control as a complex psychic function; one that is mobilized using different mechanisms which can be applied in the economy of the individual. The result of its application can be structuring, or, on the contrary, morbid and catastrophic.

The main aim of this paper is to explore the ways in which control is applied to the Self and to the Object, from the intrapsychic situation to the interpersonal relationship, the two being interconnected by reciprocity, complementarity or consonance. Another aim, arising from clinical experience, is to discuss the supposedly obsessive nature of these functions of control, and the validity of obsessive vectors as the executors both of self-control and of control over external and internal objects.

DOI: 10.4324/9781003342472-2

First, I shall make a few more preliminary comments about the self. I shall be arguing that this is the part of the personality that encompasses on the one hand, all the drives and, on the other, all the functions of the Ego: the integrative, defensive and other functions that interact with external reality. In relation to objects, I am referring to external and internalized objects, which the nucleus of the self is in a state of constant interaction with.

In point of fact, different authors use a range of lexical terms and concepts to denote this distinction between the self and internalized objects. It is not our intention to discuss this problem in any depth. Suffice to say that Melanie Klein (1959), in her explanation of the notion of the self towards the end of her work, includes all the functions of the Ego and its drives. Grinberg, L. and Grinberg, R. (1976), on the other hand, distinguish between a nucleus of the self (with the drives and functions of the Ego solidly established through fully achieved identifications) and an orbital self comprising the internalized objects, which retain their quality as internal objects, and which are at varying degrees of proximity, confusion, and antagonism or conflict with the nucleus of the self. These internal objects can evolve to the point of becoming an integral and stable part of the nucleus of the self. By contrast, the splitting of this nucleus can result in the more or less definitive shedding of fragments of internal objects. I wish to stress that in discussing the self I shall be referring to its nucleus, as opposed to the internal and external objects.

1 Psychoanalytical Perspectives Regarding the Concept of Control

The concept of control, both of the object and of the self, has undergone a series of fluctuations in psychoanalytical reflection, in accordance with the evolution of the thought of Sigmund Freud and his disciples. Thus, we could approach the problem from the following perspectives: (a) according to the theory of drives, anxiety and defence mechanisms; (b) according to a structural theory of mental functions; and (c) from the perspective of the relationship with the object.

(a) In terms of its meaning as a drive, at an intermediate moment of its evolution, according to the classical descriptions of Freud (1905) and Abraham (1924), control was driven by libido. If, at the oral stage, which is heavily imbued with sadism, libido sought the incorporation (absorption, nihilation) of the object, at the anal stage the goal was domination and possession of the object. Thus, at this stage, control did not entail the total destruction or incorporation of the object. Whether we see control as the result of an aggressive vector of the libido or as an aspect of the death drive, depending on one's theoretical preferences, what we can be sure of is that both in the clinical descriptions and in the metapsychological explanations, the different types of control are influenced by the psychosexual stages. However, what we observe in the event of reiteration of control is the

mitigation of the drive's final aim. Whatever the variations in the nature of control over the self or the object, which may have the appearance of any kind of possessiveness, of the desire for power or the need to dominate, even in the most dramatic situations, in the end this imperious drive is assuaged. In a recent study, R. Dorey argued that control is an important element of what he calls "the possessive relationship" (relation d'Emprise) (1981).In my view, whether we see control as a component of the aggression that is inherent in the libido, as a manifestation of the death drive, or as an expression of the aggression Freud associated with the self-preservative drive, it always aims at making use of the object or the self. For example, it may seek to hold on to the object or the self, to scrutinize either, in order to predict how they will behave, or to coerce, in order to restrict their actual and emotional movements. Thus, control seeks possession of the object in its outward appearance, and in its physical and mental interiority.

We could also say that, while in relation to the drive and its affects, control of the object has to do with aggression and the death drive, when seen as a defence mechanism, control possesses more positive features. In the service of the erotic drives, for example, it seeks to protect the Self and the object.

(b) Structural perspective: reciprocal control of the Self and of the Object. Not long ago, in the context of the topographical model and in relation to control of the self, one might have expressed trust or distrust in one's own unconscious. If trusting, one could allow some spontaneity, and make choices not reflexively or as a result of logical reasoning, but on the basis of an intuitive sixth sense. Trusting one's own unconscious would reflect a cordial relationship with oneself, and optimism concerning one's ability to make the right judgement in a variety of circumstances. By contrast, distrust in one's unconscious entails being alert to certain anxiety-inducing threats, having difficulty in improvising when taken by surprise and, therefore, being reserved and controlling over the never-ending flux of experience. This translates into a failure to take the initiative, as every novelty is experienced as a potential source of trauma, or in other words, as bringing the disorganization of mental stability or homeostasis. At the behavioural level, this leads the individual to be exhausted by their exercise of more or less omnipotent, control-oriented strategies, as he aims to build a precarious illusion of security.

Now, in the context of Freud's structural model, we habitually consider the means of controlling the "Id", as well as our anguish. We also tend to speak of the control exercised by the Super-Ego, the control exercised over the Super-Ego, and that exercised by the internal objects. Who controls who in this ordering or disordering of the mental apparatus? Either the subject feels that their initiative or phantasy life is being censured or watched by an internal object acting as a moral consciousness, or, by contrast, one feels, in a "first-person" mode, that one is an attentive and active subject both of one's desires and of one's self-accusations. When speaking of a cruel internal object or of the rigid imperatives of the Super-Ego, we are referring to the control of the object over the self. When, on the other hand, we speak of the mechanism of isolation, of the rejection of the internal experience and of avoidance strategies, we are referring to a kind of management of the self that forecloses new experiences both within ourselves and coming from the outside. In other words, we are referring to the self exercising control over both internalized and external objects.

(c) These mechanisms of control of the self and of objects have long been considered peculiar to neurosis and to the obsessive character. I propose to demonstrate the exercise of such mechanisms in any mental state, psychopathological or not. Needless to say, the presence of an obsessive element is not easy to delineate. Obsessive mechanisms can be found in every nosological entity and in the course of any kind of crisis, grief or traumatic episode. To my mind, the capacity to control is even more generic than that, and is actualized in a range of situations and in a wide variety of clinical disorders, when dealing with different types of anguish. Thus, I find it helpful to adjectivize "control" according to the type of control involved. In fact, this is what we do when we speak of a clearly obsessional type of control, but also of paranoid or manic control of the object, and of hysterical or perverse control of anxiety and of the object.

Besides these nosographic particularities of the mechanisms of control, it is possible to further delineate the means by which control is exerted. Thus we can distinguish *control exercised over external stimuli* (through negative hallucination, rigid attention focussing, fastidiousness, etc.) from that exercised *over internal stimuli*, such as somatic processes or the activity of the mind. Somatic processes may include denial of cenesthesia, or indifference to the corporeal processes, as opposed to opposite procedures, whereby the attention is focused on the organs and bodily functions, as in hypochondria and organoneurosis. Regarding control over mental activity, we refer to control of the emotions, of phantasies, and of thought.

As regards control that is exerted over the object, either it has to do with the concrete reality of the object, or with its contents, mental reality, desires and thoughts, which one might try to dominate through seduction, terror or guilt incitement, etc.

As soon as psychoanalysts became accustomed to dealing with schizoid defence mechanisms, and as soon as they included in their analysis of transference the anxieties associated with psychosis, and even of the autistic traits of the neurotic, they could clearly experience the vicissitudes that characterize the control of the object or parts of the object, and the control of parts of the self, which may be split off and projected into the external or internal object, the body or onto some enigmatic corner of a bizarre object.

The first descriptions of the process of projective identification by Melanie Klein (1946) and her disciples highlighted the possibility that the aim to control the object underlies such projection. Psychoanalytical research during recent decades allows us to understand more precisely both the motivations that prompt an individual to divest themselves of parts of their self or their objects, and the role that these segregated parts play in the interior of the object. And we know that the analytical technique, which focuses so meticulously on the transference–countertransference interaction, reveals the means by which the dissociated parts of the patient are projected into the analyst via the *acting in* that takes place throughout the session. In short, we have been coming to an ever more precise understanding of how this intrapsychic process known as control-oriented projective identification is externalized.

2 Clinical Assignation of Control

What follows is a series of clinical vignettes which show how control expresses itself in different relational situations. An interest in the diachronic organization of these control mechanisms has led me to view the growing complexity of their clinical expression from a genetic perspective. Thus, I have selected different observational moments from the first year of life of an infant, from the case of a young child undergoing psychoanalytical treatment and from two cases of analysis with adult patients.

In this clinical material I have deliberately left out a large amount of anamnestic data and will instead focus on passages in which the self-object conflict expresses itself in different ways depending on the external events, anxieties, and the attitude of the observer or the psychoanalyst.

In these vignettes and in the contrasts they show, it seems to me that the drive, the desire, and the practice of control of the self and the object can be understood through a series of situations which depend on different organizational moments in the individual's relationship with the object. They pertain not only to the anal state, which is regarded as a prototype of control of the object according to the sphincter model. This is not to belie the structuring value that has been attributed to the anal experience, the role that it plays in balancing the mechanisms of projection and introjection and especially the value that it has for these mechanisms as a model or scaffold for future mental functions. Thus, for example, defecation control can organize a range of experiences in the child's and adult's psychic reality, for example through: (a) control of the Self in the subject's interior, in their mental space; (b) control of the self or of parts of the self, projected onto the object; (c) control of the external object by parts of the self, incorporated at different levels of intrusion; (d) control of the internal objects by means of denial and isolation mechanisms.

2.1 Expressions of control in the systematic observation of the newborn baby

The weekly observation of the mother–infant relationship allows us to follow the development of the attitude of control. In the first weeks it is difficult to distinguish control of the self from control of the object, due to the precarious nature of their differentiation. The following are some extracts of the observations made during the first year of an infant's life.[2]

(a) *Observation N° 5 – The baby is 5 weeks old* – At this stage, the baby's control-oriented activities are expressed through his perceptive attitude, through his gestures, and through guttural sounds.

The observer notes that "... today the baby is lazy when being fed. The mother tells me that she is in a hurry because she has to leave to take one of the two baby's sisters to school. She says that the baby is probably not satisfied with the breastfeed, as it was rather rushed. While she is speaking to me, her baby is sitting on her lap and she is holding him from behind. The baby looks at me, and when I smile, he smiles back, and turns his head as if to hide his smile from me ... the mother says that perhaps he hadn't had enough milk and she begins to breastfeed him once more. With her thumb and index finger she brings her nipple to the baby's mouth; the baby turns towards his mother's breast, murmurs a little, opens his mouth and takes the nipple. Yet it doesn't seem a satisfactory situation, because he continues moving his head, loses the nipple and makes some noises. For a moment, the nipple remains in his mouth, but he does not begin to suck. I have the impression that he was touching the nipple with his tongue and moving it.

"The baby's sister then comes into the room and asks the mother something insistently. The mother answers and the baby is startled and turns his head towards his sister. When she leaves, the baby twice repeats the gesture of surprise and the look of alarm on his face, as if she had returned, though she hadn't. A little later, the baby moves his head and at the same time the mother moves her breast; the two movements are out of sync, and the baby screams again. He then starts crying as if he had wanted, in vain, to suck on the mother's nipple. The mother says it's just wind, and holds the baby over her shoulder for a good while. At first the baby's arms seem to hang limply, with his head resting on his mother's back; when the mother changes position slightly the baby suddenly fixes his mouth to the mother's shoulder-blade, as if he were looking for the nipple there ..."

> ... Before leaving, the mother lays her baby in the cot ... he is restless; with his head raised he searches the space around him, often drawing a complete circle with his chin ... When he succeeds in pressing his left hand against his mouth he is calm for a moment; when he loses his hand, he cries again and begins to look intently at a light, which calms him again.

I wish to stress a few points about this observation. There are details which are repeated throughout the observations of these first weeks: the vigilance and control-oriented responses which are particularly acute when the baby is frustrated. In the present case, these follow from the mother's hurry, the interruption of the connection with the breast upon the arrival of the baby's sister, the lack of mouth-nipple connection, etc. We notice the reaction of the baby, which consists in him fixing his gaze on his mother; it is the attempted control of the one who might leave him. He also trains his admiring gaze on her face as he perceives her during moments of gratification at the breast. The observers are able to contrast this fixed gaze, which is static and concentrated, and of a persecutory nature, with the distant look on the face of the baby in a placid state, at moments of satisfaction. Then, the observers see a trusting look that expresses the infant's good contact with the protective image of the object.

In his uncertainty and paranoid anguish at several other moments of this observation, the baby's gaze is focused on a single fixed point, a radiant point of light. Now, this object has become the centre, the equivalent of the nipple. Besides his wish to control, which is a reaction to his frustration and anguish, this observation shows that the baby is beginning to practise a repetitive manoeuvre which, to my mind, prefigures a control-oriented ritual which we shall encounter weeks later; a manoeuvre that will be practised explicitly and consciously. But the notes for week five already show that the baby repeats an attitude of surprise and vigilance when a danger – his sister disturbing the breastfeed – has obviously passed. This reminds us of anxiety-related control, as in phobia, for example, through the active search for an object that triggers anxiety.

(b) Observation N° 15 – The baby is three months and three weeks old. – "... At the beginning of the observation, the mother says that the baby has a cold, has not slept well, and is very irritable. Once at his mother's breast, he begins to feed calmly. His sisters are making a lot of noise. When the baby turns to look at them, he loses the nipple. On realizing this, he reacts quickly and easily recovers it. During the six or eight minutes of the breastfeed, every time he hears a noise, he turns his head. He seems unconcerned by the little girls who are still playing noisily. The act of turning his head and then this quick recovery of the mother's nipple has become a game which he keeps repeating even after the little girls have stopped playing ..."

> When the mother gave the baby fruit puree, he ate it with no problem, but whereas during the breastfeed his feet were still, now he moves them excitedly ... When the mother left the room and asked me to keep my eye on him, he had one leg on top of the other, and his knuckles in his mouth, pressing them hard against his gums ...

In this way we can see that control by direct contact calms the baby when the presence of the object seems threatened. This auto-erotic retreat, when the mother leaves, serves to maintain the psychic homeostasis. As regards the game (the loss and retrieval of the nipple), it seems to me that this has a defensive purpose, following the traumatic experience of loss of the nipple, and at the same time it provides functional training.

(c) Observation N° 34 – 9 months. – I shall only describe two fragments of this observation, which was carried out just a few weeks after weaning. This experience deeply affected both the baby and the mother, to the extent that the mother preferred someone else to feed her son.

When the observer arrives, the baby is engrossed in a repetitive game. He has a cup with a plastic beak, full of fruit juice. After holding it carelessly for a while he drops it onto the ground, then he starts smiling and sucks his thumb, still with a broad smile on his face. The housemaid picks up the cup and offers it to the baby again, trying to get him to drink the fruit juice, but the game begins again, and the cup once more falls to the floor. The baby seems to be eloquently showing us that the drink is disgusting, but his thumb is delicious. After repeating this game a number of times, the baby gets angry with the maid and throws the cup away from himself. ... When his mother crosses the room, the child, still refusing to eat, bursts into tears ... Instead of eating he tries to suck the plate ... the mother feels obliged to intervene and the child rests his head between her breasts and begins to calm down ... Then we see how he runs his mouth along his mother's arm and begins to suck it ... and presses his fingers into her skin ... The mother tries to distract him, but the baby takes his penis with his left hand and pulls at it from time to time ... Later he stands up on his mother's lap and shouts triumphantly before continuing to suck her arm. When his mother lays him on the rug, he starts pulling at his penis again ..."

(d) Observation N° 41 – The child is one year and one week old. – "At the start of the observation the child is in the garden with the maid. He is sitting down but asks to be carried. He becomes more and more impatient, and the maid decides to take him to the playroom. She gives him a doll, and he takes a particular interest in its eyes, but then he tires of it. The maid then gives him a mechanical toy, then encourages him to look through the window at a cat crossing the patio. The child soon loses interest and the maid then offers him a little telephone, three plastic cups and some other toys ... Then he notices some of his sister's toys. The maid sits him on her lap and shows him some pictures in a picture-book. "Look at this cat!" The child touches the animal's mouth with his thumb, and then does the same with the other pictures. Suddenly he seems startled by something, and stands up on the maid's lap. She holds him against her chest and starts to sing a song about horses galloping, while she pretends to gallop with the child on her lap. ... The child then reaches out to pick up some other books, but the maid doesn't let him, leading the child to protest. The doorbell rings and the maid leaves the room; the child starts crying; I come a bit closer and try to distract him with the telephone. The child sucks his thumb and looks at me with an expression of suspicion. There are biscuit crumbs on the floor and he starts picking them up with

his left hand. He becomes totally engrossed in this activity of picking up the crumbs. Then he rubs his eyes, all the while keeping his left thumb in his mouth …. Just then the maid comes back. The child cries but calms down quickly when she picks him up. He tries to put a foot on her chest as if he wanted her to piggy-back him, but she doesn't let him; then he pulls so hard on her blouse that he pulls off a button. Both of them laugh loudly. The child wets the maid's cheek with his mouth … He tries to bite her back; she laughs and presses her head against the child's belly … They continue these arousing games for some time. The maid squeals while rubbing her nose against the child's belly. The games become more and more violent, the child bites her and tries to put one of his legs between the girl's breasts, he pulls her blouse and drools over it …"

> … When the mother arrives, the child is overjoyed and heads for her as fast as he can. When she picks him up in her arms, he presses his head against her neck … Then she feeds him, with some difficulty, and the spoon sometimes goes too far into his mouth … The mother gives him an empty spoon while she continues feeding him with the other spoon. The child holds out his arm with the empty spoon till it almost touches his mother's mouth, and as he does so he opens his mouth wide and receives a spoonful of food …

If we compare this with earlier observations, we see that the control of the object has become more nuanced. The child also demonstrates somewhat better self-control. His manic control of objects develops rapidly, and shifts from one object to another. He is also better able to represent his internal discomfort, and his anguish is controlled by dissociative mechanisms. In this way, for example, the child can offload onto the maid the pain of separation, while the mother can sustain the phantasy of being a good object. This allows a good contact to be re-established when the mother returns. It is curious that when the child is alone with the observer, after the maid leaves, he is calm at first, but when the observer speaks to him, he becomes restless, as if he notices that the voice of his mother, undoubtedly unique, contrasts with the voice of this stranger. We also see the containment of anguish in the amazing game with the spoon: it highlights progress with respect to comparable situations several months before, when the child tried to resolve his anguish by means of fusion with the object. When the anguish of fragmentation caused by the sudden loss of the external object (the maid who leaves) increases, the child tries to control and reintegrate parts of himself, projected into the biscuit crumbs, by carefully gathering them up.

What is also obvious in this observation is the difference between the relationship with the mother and with the maid. The latter does not know how to contain the child's anxiety and engages in complicit masturbatory and manic arousal, through the accumulation of toys and the nature of the games. By contrast, the mother knows how to contain the child without arousing him too much. The mother's relationship with her child is a tender one, while that with the maid is frankly eroticized. The child's control of the object through projective identification also occurs in the course of this observation, through other means of intrusion. The child is also beginning to use words. His vocalization, which is beginning to acquire meaning, is understood by the adults around him to have more precise nuances than his former screaming and crying could reveal.

(e) Comments on the observations. – In these four cameos we have tried to show the progress of the baby's attempts to manage his different types of anguish. At the beginning, the same control manoeuvre is applied equally to the Self as to the Object, given their lack of differentiation. Thus, the recovery of the object via intense fusional contact, by oral incorporation, by means of intrusion, or the fixed gaze, etc. ensures the recovery of emotional homeostasis and, with it, incipient control of the self. The repetitive, seemingly ludic manoeuvres, in which the loss and recovery of the object are parodied, should be viewed in the light of Freud's observations (Freud 1920) concerning the mastery of traumatic experience through repetition.

In the course of the different observations, we have seen these manoeuvres in all their complexity. Indeed they grew in complexity in proportion to the development of the infant's perceptual-motor functions and his capacity for symbolization. When this capacity is actualized, the infant's representation of the self and the object goes beyond the initial auto-erotic resources, beyond his own body and that of the mother. Substitutive people and things will form part of the child's ever richer expressive and representative toolkit. Self-control and control of the object will be practised in more and more meaningful ludic situations. In all such situations, the mechanisms of dissociation, projection, displacement, etc. facilitate, as we have seen, control of anguish, of self-arousal and impulses. The control of the object also becomes more varied and nuanced; to this end, projective identification becomes more efficient with each new enrichment of the child's psycho-physical functionalism.

2.2 *Control in the psychoanalytical clinic*

In the following clinical vignettes, I have also selected material that will serve to illustrate this theme. They concern some very different patients at different moments during their psychoanalytical treatment.

(a) Case N° 1 – This child was eight years old when he began psychoanalytical treatment with me. At that age, attitudes of control are much more complex than those discussed in relation to the observations of the baby. They cannot be reduced to the direct action that we typically see in precocious psychoanalytical treatment with children under five. In the case I shall describe, these attitudes are manifest during play, in verbal

expression and also, needless to say, in gestures and posture, in direct action and in any other kind of acting out.

The treatment was prompted by difficulties the child was experiencing at school, such as attention dispersion and reading problems. It was also motivated by concern about certain character traits which, due to their exaggerated nature, were a cause of concern for the parents: obstinacy, jealous rivalry with siblings (an older brother who had suffered a psychotic episode and a well-balanced younger sister), indifference to parental requirements, coldness in the event of being punished, capricious bulimia, encopresis, arrogance, and persistence in errors that led to bitter failure. The child was refractory when his parents tried to reason with him, especially where they were insistent. As regards his anamnesis, he repeatedly recalled traumatic episodes: several surgical interventions to correct his strabismus when he was two years old; and his great suffering at the hands of his brother, who had tortured him physically and mentally and had incited him to masturbatory practices.

From the first sessions the child experienced an intense transference, such as we often find among much younger infants. He very quickly expressed a fear that I might confuse him with his brother. In his games at that time he often reiterated this worry. For example, he would bury little objects in a lump of plasticine and then I had to guess, from the size, the position of each buried object. Then he would put these objects (little glass balls, bits from the box of a toy construction set, etc.) inside a castle he had made with different materials, and the same guessing game would ensue. In this game, finally there was just one piece left inside the castle. The child would also take an interest in the different drawers of the table where he used to play, and would ask if all the drawers were the same inside, and if the other children I treated had the same toys in their respective drawers, etc.

In order to secure my full and exclusive recognition, the child's behaviour was extremely docile and cooperative, to the point of seduction. He actively accepted my interpretations, was gentle with me, and took pleasure in imitating my gestures and adopting certain phrases he heard me using. However, the weekend separations disrupted the illusion of being that only child. Nevertheless, he made an effort to accept interpretations that highlighted his attacks against me as someone who was abandoning him, which he felt as the mother leaving him to be with the father. One day he drew a snow-capped hill: his father was skiing on it and fell. When I interpreted that this drawing conveyed his aggressive feelings towards me, which were often concealed by his docility and cooperation, his immediate reaction was to draw another hill with his father calmy and safely skiing down. But then he would build a castle out of plasticine with a single small wooden cube inside it. It was then easy to show him that this castle represented the reward he expected for his docility and his willingness to erase his father's accident. I also showed him his anguish if a good, peaceful relationship with me was not re-established immediately. On other occasions the seduction was effected by other more tender, ingenuous means, such as when he represented himself as a little chicken walking on four legs, to which he gave the names of the four days of the week when he came to see me. This comparison of the four sessions with the four legs was a flattering tribute, in that the sessions did indeed seem to stimulate him in hitherto static situations, such as performance at school. The external effects of this initial symbiosis were confirmed by the family, who considered the treatment to be a spectacular success; but in fact, the movement had been very regressive.

My interpretation of the child's seductive behaviour and of the anguish which led to this confusion with me, and the way in which he worked through his experience during the summer holiday, enabled him to overcome his intense inclination towards massive projective identification. It also enabled him to tolerate, not without some resentment, the loss of the therapeutic idyll of the first months. He also reacted with an acting out in relation to his brother, which he described to me with pride. It led me to feel that, given the good rapport he usually had with his brother, he was actually suggesting he no longer needed me. He also resorted to "magical" scenarios; in the sessions he would pretend to be a conjuror. He would practise rituals to transform himself into a desired object. These games would extend beyond the sessions with actions whose extravagance surprised his family. With some of these rituals, his intention was to ensure a certain course of events; for example, by marking objects with saliva, he could made them docile and predictable. At other times his need to emulate and simulate took a negative form: if he could detect a tiny defect in someone, that person became his equal. He never missed a single slip of the tongue on my part; on other occasions he was particularly attentive to the smallest details of my consulting room, of the people who came in and left the flat. But when his anguish mounted these resources were not sufficient, and he would resort to even stronger magical methods: making coins of ever increasing value out of cardboard or plasticine, giving himself the best marks in his class at school, awarding himself trophies in competitions with me, which he would dramatize by drawing a table-soccer match on large sheets of paper. A clear understanding of this situation, with his insistence on recovering at all costs a manic triumph, became all the more necessary when his jealousy towards his brother intensified while he was making obvious progress.

Later the child began to exhibit an arrogant, albeit more reserved attitude. He would spend entire sessions reading books or children's magazines; in this way he was showing me his contempt; that he didn't need me, and that, by contrast, he was enthused by his reading. He was also showing me that he had succeeded; that now he had acquired automatic reading skills, which had been an important aim of the therapy. On other days his attitude was very closed, and he would only catch a ball, throw it against the wall, pick it up and then begin again. He seemed totally indifferent to my interpretations, though at times he would pretend that he was concentrating on his reading, and steal furtive glances at me to see what I was doing while I was sitting in silence. I had also interpreted this dedication to reading as the construction of an impenetrable space – a replica of the imaginary castle which I had forced him to abandon. I also interpreted that it was a humble recognition by him that he had made progress; that he was no longer the same backward pupil he was at the start of treatment. The repetitive games with the ball will be understood as a means of ensuring the return of the object. When the ball fell into my lap or brushed past my glasses, I said that it was only in this way that he could again get close to me. I was the ball he had let go of, yet he could continue reach me an to express very different feelings: seeking refuge in my lap or attacking my eyes so that I would become blind, as he was, to the rage that kept him at a distance. Following my interpretations, the games would continue with certain variations, sometimes more intensely, as if in an attempt to end all mental activity.

What I wish to stress with this material is the contrast between the control directed at the interior of the object, which is accompanied by a phantasy of a massive invasion via projective identification, and the control of the object with minimal intrusion, using various techniques in a process of trial and error, such as verification of the distance between the self and object, and vigilance. Alongside this more precise and meticulous control, there was another gratuitous, magical form of control that the child used where a more invasive kind of control failed. This was based on realistic knowledge of the object, and has been described by L. Grinberg (1966) as adaptive, in his brilliant study of the transition in control-oriented relationships, from magical variations of control to more adaptive kinds.

In the case I have just commented on, at the start of the treatment we find the first control variant, which was attempted by means of seduction. It included a mimesis which reinforced the child's illusion of an almost fusional reciprocal belonging with me, which only reiterated interpretation was able to diminish. The control then took on more rigid features, but became less confused and therefore more realistic.

(b) *Case N° 2* – The patient, whom I shall call A, is a typical case of obsessional neurosis with very obvious manifestations from early infancy, aggravated by a particularly traumatic pubertal crisis. He was 25 years old when therapy began, and even then had a brilliant and privileged career. A specialist in biochemistry, he devoted a large part of his time to working in the laboratory of a prestigious company's research department. He presented an unmistakeable example of "folie du doute", especially in respect of religious matters. He doubted everything concerning sin, faith, beliefs and the sacred mysteries. Helpless in the face of the deluge of questions that he was formulating to himself, his rage bordered on

blasphemy. This would trigger endless internal debates about the automatic, spontaneous or voluntary character of cursing; new debates which
exhausted themselves, or led to feelings of depersonalization. In his despair at not being able to resolve these doubts on his own, he felt he had no
choice but to consult his spiritual director, who had to certify that he had
not sinned, that he had certainly not sinned, and that it was even impossible for him to sin. But that only put the patient's mind at rest momentarily. Soon, his feeling that he had pressured the priest prompted him to
seek fresh counsel, in which the priest had to reassure him that he had not
felt pressured in any way. Sometimes the patient would react by treating
the priest as a heretic, because if he was telling him that he couldn't sin, he
was either denying his condition as a free agent, or regarding him either
as saintly or as mentally incapable.

The patient was very irritated by the first interpretations I proposed,
which focused on his thoroughness in pondering the meaning of my
words, and whether there was anything heretical in them. He would often
wonder whether I was a believer, a practising Catholic or an atheist. When
I told him that what he was really asking was whether I was the eluci-
dator in our work, he tried to find a transactional explanation that would
satisfy him for a moment. According to him, there were two types of guilt:
moral guilt and psychological guilt; the first was a matter for spiritual
direction and I had no reason to intervene; psychological guilt was my
sphere, but then it was unconscious guilt, and therefore free of sin. On the
rare occasions when his anxiety concerning absurd guilt had a realistic
basis, his distress was extreme. When that happened, either he himself
would offer a crazy interpretation whereby everything could be explained
in terms of childhood trauma and the errors that he had been subjected to
by his educators, or he would increase sessions with his spiritual directors.
Depending on the nature of the sin he felt he might have committed, he
would consult one director or another; thus, for example, a biologist priest
assured him that he was not responsible for any "micro abortions" when
he approved, in his laboratory, the commercialization of a contraceptive
product. Another priest, a specialist in canon law, had to state whether or
not the patient had committed a sin that incurred excommunication.
Another, a philosopher, had to explain to him to what extent his metaphysi-
cal doubts amounted to heresy. The interpretation of these problems as
attempts to isolate his thinking into compartments led to unbearable anguish
in the sessions with me. The patient would reject, with further compartmentalization, my attempts to show him a more meaningful and comprehensible
holistic picture. He would react with new dissociations and an increase in
doubt, and then would perform calming rituals, attend further consultations
with his spiritual directors, and send rather pathetic, self-pitying letters to his
parents in America. If I momentarily succeeded in correcting his tendency to
compartmentalize, he showed me by his agitation and increasing anguish
that I was responsible for his worsening condition.

At such moments, he would not allow me to interrupt the flow of his words. I had to listen to his description of his faults and to the most absurd sacrilegious doubts that he allowed himself to entertain. He would tell me with great anxiety that he urgently needed to produce a verbal recomposition, using precise words, of prayers or unequivocal invocations, and here "unequivocal" meant "with no parasitical blasphemy". The fact that I listened acquiescently to his entire speech had for him the magical meaning of a reawakening in which he felt totally pious and innocent. On such occasions, the whole session acquired for him the value of a propitiatory ritual. In fact, the persecution being carried out by an accusing, implacable, and tyrannical internal object, albeit an aberrant one, was mitigated through an externalization whereby this terrible object was dispersed amongst the spiritual directors and the psychoanalyst; the directors and I were becoming judges whom he was in control of. At such times, I was a tamed fragment of his terrible Super-Ego. I remember saying to him that when he obliged me to quietly listen to his propitiatory confession, I was no longer either a spiritual director or an analyst, but a little altar boy who had to say "Amen" to everything.

When my interpretations seemed inopportune, (and the greater his suffering the more likely this was), his speech became all the more compact, rigid, and syntactically rigorous. The fear of a swear word slipping into the flow of his thoughts, and especially his fear of uttering a swear word, was related to the fear of something extremely toxic slipping out from inside himself. This led him to speak of his own pseudo-masturbatory practices. In saying that they were "pseudo" he meant that they were not voluntary: they happened while he was half-asleep, with his hands tied to prevent him from touching his genitals. As in so many other cases, the whole weight of the guilt fell on what was most unintentional and concrete, on whether or not an emission of sperm had taken place. The notion of a potential explosion of catastrophic effects expressed itself in all kinds of anecdotal contents. The patient felt hurt when we considered that the destructive aspect of his expulsive impulse did not lie in a drop of sperm or saliva, or in the initial syllable of a blasphemous word, but in the uninterrupted torrent of his speech, which made it impossible for me to understand him; or in the rigour and precision of his exposition, which caused him to lose track of his science in the broad sense, and, at the same time, of its meaning.

At times I lost patience with his ambiguous and euphemistic way of referring to an occasional swear word that might have assaulted his thoughts. When I referred to the swear word in my intervention and expressed it verbally, he would immediately accuse me of irreverence and insensitivity to the importance he attached to sacred things. In fact, he was making me blaspheme and then introjecting me as a blasphemer. Then it was his turn to take on the role of moralistic and rigorous Super-Ego.

The fear of falling into the sin of cruelty in his practice of animal dissection and especially of indirectly favouring "micro abortions" by working in a laboratory which developed certain hormonal products, reached absurd levels. By displacing his anxiety, he ended up completely losing any sense of personal responsibility. When I said that the impossible and eccentric guilt he experienced on account of the "micro abortions" was a substitute for the effective abortion he inflicted on our communication during the sessions, he would protest. He realized, perceptively, that he had exceeded the limits of my patience. Even more than the fear of my pronouncing a technical judgement, another terror arose in his mind: that of being excommunicated. This penalty is imposed specifically on those who contribute to abortion, or try to seduce a confessor or assault a priest. Had he randomly struck a priest on the street during a demonstration, or while playing with a ball as a child, he wondered? Had he spat out a piece of the host when sneezing after taking communion? These were the equivalents, in terms of their obsessional quality, of the attacks being made on the possibilities of the session. Other such attacks included his late arrivals, missed sessions or spending the whole time on detailed, self-pitying descriptions of the vagaries of the night before. I myself was surprised by my repeated interpretations, for in the here-and-now of the session, the micro-abortions took place when, totally ignoring me, he attempted to prevent me from being a free presence at his side, with desires and intentions that were different from his.

It was only after verifying several times his need to silence me and prevent me taking any initiative, that he acknowledged, with regret, the control he was exercising over me, and how fearful he was of what I might say, which led him not to want to hear anything new from me. He began to feel sincerely sorry about his phantasy of "curaring" me (curare was a substance that he had used in his laboratory); that is to say, of causing, through his style of relating to me, disconnections in my thoughts which ensured my immobility. This "curare" phantasy corresponds fully to the projective identification of invading the object with the aim of possessing and controlling it.

In this case, control was expressed in different ways, but the mechanisms used in all cases were based on dissociation, disavowal, isolation, obsession with detail, compartmentalization of problems, idea–affect isolation, metaphoric–literal meaning, external–internal conflict, etc. The same symptoms, such as obsessional doubting, enabled him to control himself and his objects: that is to say, on the one hand, through doubt the patient controlled his impulses, but also, out of resentment, he scrutinized the obvious attitude and inner feelings of the analyst.

If exerting control was expressed in case N° 1 (the newborn child) through the abundant use of motricity, it was much more subtle in case N° 2, where it was expressed mainly with recourse to language. For this reason, in this latter case the correspondence between the control of

external objects and the situation of extreme internal tension in a reciprocal control of the internalized "superegoist" self and object, was much
clearer.

(c) Case N° 3 – To conclude these clinical vignettes, I shall present the
case of a psychotic patient in analysis who exemplifies the types of control
that are associated with the acute period, and in moments of reorganization after, a catatonic "bouffée". Rather than present a systematic account
of the case, I shall limit myself to saying by way of context that she is a
24-year-old patient suffering from schizophrenia who, at the start of psychoanalysis with me, had suffered two acute psychotic episodes which
were treated with electroconvulsive shock therapy and neuroleptic drugs.
She had been recovering, but with severe inhibitions in her intellectual
and relational life.

When we were still in the first months of the analysis, certain adverse
circumstances caused a spectacular relapse. First, the relationship with the
social worker who was looking after her came to an abrupt end. Then, a
relative, the psychologist who had encouraged her to begin treatment, had
to leave the country. The proximity of the Christmas holidays and the
marriage of her sister were then the last straws in this series of circumstances, which resulted in a full-blown catatonic agitation syndrome,
requiring her to be hospitalized urgently.

In the first sessions I conducted in the clinic, the patient could only express
herself extraverbally. She was in a state of total mutism and corporeal rigidity. She was completely unresponsive to every stimulus, only altering her
bodily posture slightly whenever I made a comment. Some days later she
would respond with occasional furtive looks. After a week of daily sessions,
the patient would react to my presence a little more and, besides, I was able
to observe her reactions in greater detail. There were clear changes in her
bodily position in response to my interpretations, which, little by little, were
being received with more and more normal positions.

At first I limited myself to describing to her what I observed in her, but
then I interpreted her immobility in terms of the feeling of imminent cat-
astrophe that she had conveyed to me in the weeks before her crisis. Her
immobility was interpreted as a way of stopping everything; as expressing
her wish that nothing would happen either around her or inside her. At
other moments, if she dared to look at me, I said that in her immobility
and her silence she felt far away from every kind of violence, in contrast
with her agitated experience that preceded her admission to hospital. I
spoke to her about the terror she felt in the face of any kind of change:
absences, holidays, her sister's wedding, etc. If everything stopped
moving, this meant that she no longer felt desire, or feelings of loss, or
need of anyone.

When she emerged from her mutism, she would make little exclama-
tions which, apparently, were not addressed to me. A tense, and
obviously scrutinizing attention, was mobilized by minor adventitious

incidents; a barking dog, birds twittering in the clinic garden, the sound of a coach braking. She would lose her immobility and listen, alarmed, turning towards the source of the sound. Her look was imploring, as if she were about to burst into tears. All this meant progress, and broadened the range of interpretative possibilities. A few days later, these external persecutory elements began to take on a human character. She seemed to me to understand my interpretation when I said that her immobility was a way of avoiding accidents, ruptures or fits of anger within herself, even though she related it to external agents. A further step was her verbalization of her fear of dogs and birds, which she said barked or sang in consonance with her thoughts. I understood that I, for her, was a noise, a dog's bark or birdsong, speaking in a certain correspondence with her thoughts. There was a beginning of meaning in this concrete music that my words represented for her during those days. A little later, she began to listen to me more attentively and to stare at me; then she said that the birds and dogs sang and barked in accordance with what we were saying.

Her eroticization of our relationship was restrained, but obvious. Then she would include me in her self-references: "We look at each other, they recognise us, they persecute us". Despite everything, there was a reconnection with reality, and the patient could return home three weeks after being admitted.

We resumed the sessions in my consulting room. Her catatonic state became more and more hysterical. Her corporeal expression of anxiety became increasingly nuanced. She would dress provocatively, and negligently, emphasizing her prominent breasts and very narrow waist. Her lips were painted with excess lipstick, her dress was wrinkled and dirty, and her gait rather unsteady. In the course of the session she would get up to see if anyone was hiding behind the curtain. She would say that the passers-by were watching her as she came up to the consulting room. On the days when she didn't have a session, she thought that she found me in lots of different places. She felt I made the traffic lights change when she had to cross the street. According to her, I must have been directing the traffic like a rather moody guardian angel who made her think of everything she had to do. But then suddenly she would say that she was in a huge hostile city, scarcely knowing where she was or where she was going.

My fragmented interpretation of the modes of expression of her fear of mental collapse, of losing her identity, and of her need for a parasitical or confused relationship with me, led her to consciously and increasingly eroticize the treatment. This eroticization I interpreted as meeting an urgent need for projective identification. The sudden awareness of her desire for a concrete relationship with me, her difficulty in tolerating the weekend separations, her dreams of a sexual relationship with me with no masking of her feelings, led to a surprising acting out on her part: the patient began a romantic liaison with a university student of her age. The transference was obviously dissociative, which facilitated verbal expression. Encouraged by her family, the patient discreetly resumed her social life and took on a job in a warehouse. In her sessions, she protected herself against live contact with me by means of rituals and neutral accounts of the events of the day. That said, she allowed these rituals and accounts to be penetrated by interpretation, and she was able to acknowledge, with great emotion, her desperate attempt to take refuge from a sense of imminent collapse. Then she told me how her defensive resources were, to her mind, pathetic and disgusting: she had to place her purse at a precise distance from her chair; she had to touch on several occasions all the contents of her handbag; she found it hard to let go of the ashtray she had just used; and she was afraid of an explosion which would happen who knows where, whilst all the while she wondered whether she had this absurd notion because of recent news about terrorist attacks. Sometimes she felt duty-bound to read everything. She complained about feeling obliged to look away when things were happening imperceptibly around her.

All these actions or verbal expressions occurred at a decisive moment in her relationship with me. For example, her fear of explosions was intensified at moments when she felt very confused with regard to me, or was desiring me. The compulsion to read everything was expressed at moments when she was not listening to me and could not receive anything through her ears. When the evacuative style of expression predominated, the compulsion to perceive everything seemed to be an attempt to compensate for the void resulting from the massive projections of aspects of her self.

During the course of a session dealing with these confusional anxieties and with her difficulty in differentiating between reality and her phantasies, she told me she had recently been working with her father's scissors, and that it had suddenly occurred to her that there might be an explosion in the neighbouring quarry. We could see that she experienced using the scissors, a symbol for the capacity for discrimination, as if she were materially using my mind. "Despite everything", she told me, "everything is foggy and murky … I just read that a soldier had a double kidney transplant … They were the kidneys of another soldier". When I told her that for her to function mentally it seemed necessary to her for someone else to lose their capacity to think, and that using my thoughts was like stealing two kidneys from me, the patient replied: "Can't you hear the dogs starting to bark?" This was her way of protesting.

Immediately after one weekend, she broke a long silence to say to me: "I still get flustered by the same things, keeping a close eye on the objects in my briefcase … Yesterday I was watching television with my family, and the screen was clearly changing according to the tone of my conversation with my parents and brothers; at other times it changed according to my thoughts and the changes were especially to the colour tone and the lines that appeared on the screen … It was all very strange …

In any case, you control everything: the television, the planes, everything is so strange and chaotic". I told her, in fact, that everything is in chaos in her head and that she is not looking far through the television, nor is she thinking about me, who is far away from her from Friday to Monday; quite the opposite, in fact, she and her family are being watched by me, and I control them. When she thinks like this, she has me back beside her again, and she doesn't miss me.

In this case, the types of control are aberrant. Adaptive control is very often missing. The mechanisms of magic, omnipotent control predominate, and this happens at the expense of the patient's most elemental perceptive functions. The patient oscillated, at the most critical moments, between explosions, atomization and confusional anxiety. The defensive control she deployed was more anxiogenic than anxiolytic, and she swung from one pole of anguish to another.

The object control phantasies were applied to my body and my mind, and translated into her mimicking my gestures and my voice; at other times the control was transferred to objects in my office; we also saw how she would project this control to other people and animals. Some of the obsessive rituals I have described metaphorized the control of the external object, that of the lost object, her mental turmoil and fear of confusion.

One could speak in this case, following Bion (1958), of control of the object by hallucination. In her delirium, the patient feels under my unrelenting vigilance, but, at the same time, the delirium and hallucination provide her with a kind of omniscience: she becomes aware of what she believes to be my manoeuvres and intentions. We might say that when her anguish was at its peak, the control of the internal and external object was expressed, as M. Klein explains, through an extreme form of catatonic stupor. Needless to say, it would be abusive to speak of an obsessive state in the case of someone who is catatonic. I have provided this clinical material rather to demonstrate the metamorphosis of obsessive patterns of control as responses to the most archaic anxieties.

3 Obsessive Nature or Universal Character of Control

The variety of types of control discussed may appear in any syndrome. It is not possible to believe in a specificity more typical of a particular nosological entity. If the first descriptions indicated greater likelihood, in cases of obsessive character neurosis, the path that I have just traced in describing this collection of heterogeneous clinical situations, to which we could add even more examples of perverse or manic control, etc., shows that the spectre of phantasies and actions in the service of the control of the self and of the object extends to all cases, with a use which ranges from the most structuring aims to the most elemental defence mechanisms. A magnificent study contrasting mechanisms of control can be found in the article by R. Dorey (1981) on the possessive relationship, in which he compares the modalities of perverse and obsessive organization in the subjugation, manipulation, and control of the object.

The generalization of these mechanisms even inclines me to think that every defence mechanism could be aimed at control, or at least could have control-like effects such as limitation and coercion in respect of the expansion of the self and the objects. That said, I do not think that all defences can be described as controlling, nor do I think that their defensive purpose can be reduced to control. On the contrary, it is a matrix of many learning experiences, and serves the aim of maintaining good mental functioning. In this sense, the verification or testing of reality could be included as a form of control. We could also say the same of the signal-anxiety and of the regulation of the primary process by the secondary process.

What happens in obsessional neurosis is that the need to control the self and the object becomes more compelling and conscious, more acknowledged by the subject. By contrast, in other clinical case studies, control is more automatic and more likely to be denied. That would explain why from early on, control-oriented motivations and intentions were associated with obsessive states. Patients of this kind oscillate in their unstable equilibrium between paranoid and confusional anxiety on the one hand and depressive anxiety on the other. Their interminable struggle with the recognition of guilt is sustained with measures of control which preserve the familiar dissociations of the idea and the affect, the isolations between one experience and the other, and between one internal and external object and the other. In case A, this translates symptomatically into a dramatic oscillation between the various alternatives to constant doubt.

4 Final Considerations. Control and Freedom

The aspects of control of which I have been speaking find clinical expression within the context of the therapeutic situation. As analysts, we observe and suffer these as forms of resistance: resistance to the transference, resistance to free association, and resistance to insight. By means of different resources which we experience as obstacles to our therapeutic aims, the patient proceeds: through detailed ruminations, bringing random fragments of his experience, vindicatory rationalizations, repetitions, and rigidly prudent attitudes. All of this triggers the analyst countertransferential reactions which we can often barely tolerate. When this happens, the sense of our thought being blocked makes us feel caught in a trap laid by the patient. The danger is, as always, not realizing what is happening, with the risk of falling into one of two equally sterile alternatives: either we are prisoners of a projective counter-identification, assuming and acting the projection of a guilt-manipulating Super-Ego, in which case we become moralists trying at all costs, for example, to interpret the "obsessive trick", or the evasive displacements; or we want to demonstrate that the solid foundation and meaning of what the patient experiences is absurd; or we fall prey to collusion, and become implicated in the mimetic adoption of the rationalizing style of the patient.

This complicity is all the more likely to ensure the marginalization of the affects. Since the patient is very agile in his or her intellectualization, they prompt us to examine too closely the content of what they bring, at the expense of gaining an understanding of the attitude or atmosphere of the session and, in short, of their very effective acting out. Only the acknowledgement of our countertransference can enable us to escape the limitations in which we find ourselves, and to recover our freedom of thought or free-floating attention so that its continued practice can be introjected by the patient in the form of ever freer association.

In fact, free-floating attention and free association are counterpoints to the pathological control which is exercised, in different degrees, over the self and on the object. Having said that, control and freedom are not mutually exclusive antagonists. On the contrary, their commensalism can produce a fertile synergy. As Green reminded us (Marseilles Symposium, European Fed. 1984), if the patient is to maintain any degree of freedom at all, his illness must remain at least to some extent controllable by him. Similarly, in order to preserve the function of containment in the sense that Bion (1970) meant it, the analyst, or indeed mother, must remain vigilant and maintain an adequate level of control over him or herself. Bion's recommendation that the analyst acquire a good attitude by freeing themselves of memory and desire, makes us totally present with the patient, even at the mercy of the present, without the burden of past experience, of theoretical prejudices, even without the burden of our most recent past with the patient. Without past, without memory, but also without desires. That is to say, without envisaging any precise future, with no trajectory in mind for our patient which might present itself as desirable. We know perfectly well that being in the here-and-now of our relationship with the patient is not a stable position, but one which can be lost and regained at every moment. A benevolent vigilance of our need for security and our desires in the form of therapeutic yearnings, will enable the control and the freedom to achieve a fortunate outcome.

Notes

1 1975 (Published in *Revista Catalana de Psicoanàlisi*, vol. II, no.1, 1985).
2 These observations were made by Terttu Eskelinen as part of the research material for a study group led by Ester Bick in London, 1970–1972. I gained access to this material by courtesy of the participants.

Bibliography

Abraham, K. (1924) Breve estudio del desarrollo de la libido a la luz de los trastornos mentales, in *Psicoanálisis clínico*, Ed. Hormé.
Bion, W. R. (1958) On hallucination, *International Journal of Psycho-Analysis*, vol. 39, no. 5.
Bion, W. R. (1970) *Attention and Interpretation*, Tavistock Publications, London.

Dorey, R. (1981) La relation d'emprise, *Nouvelle Revue de Psychanalyse*.

Freud, S. (1905) *Three Essays on Sexuality. Standard Edition*, vol. VII.

Freud, S. (1913) *The Disposition to Obsessional Neurosis. Standard Edition*, vol. XII.

Freud, S. (1920) *Beyond the Pleasure Principle. Standard Edition*, vol. XVII.

Freud, S. (1937) *Analysis Terminable and Interminable. Standard Edition*, vol. XXIII.

Grinberg, L. (1966) The relationship between obsessive mechanisms and a state of self-disturbance: Depersonalization. *International Journal of Psycho-Analysis*, vol. 47, nos 2–3.

Grinberg, L. and Grinberg, R. (1976) *Identidad y cambio*. Ed. Paidós.

Klein, M. (1946) Notes on some schizoid mechanisms, in *The Writings of Melanie Klein*, vol. III.

Klein, M. (1959) Our adult world and its roots in infancy, in *The Writings of Melanie Klein*, vol. III.

3 Literary Process and Psychoanalytical Process[1]

Pere Folch Mateu

1 Analogies and Contrasts

The aim of the following consideration of psychoanalytical process and "literary process" is to highlight the similarities and the contrasts between two very different types of interpersonal relationships: on the one hand, the relationship between the psychoanalyst and his patient, and on the other, the relationship between the author (or the text) and the reader (or listener, at, for example, a public reading, or member of the audience at a theatrical performance). The analogy implied by the title of this paper invites us to consider the most salient features of either process, and the most obvious correspondences between them, however striking are the differences that distinguish these communicative situations. For example, analysis, the result of a prior agreement, is precise in terms of time and place, whereas the literary encounter, by contrast, is so imprecise, polymorphous and diverse. It takes place between the author, the text and the reader, a reader who, as we shall see, may be an individual or a formal group (in the case of a theatrical performance), or anonymous and dispersed (in the case of a television broadcast).

In view of the enormous disparity between these two contexts, does it make any sense to explore the coincidences, the parallelisms and the contrasts between them? To establish a rationale for doing so, we should first explain what we mean by psychoanalytical process, a concept initially developed by Freud, but which has been more fully conceptualized by contemporary psychoanalysts. By contrast, the term "literary process" has not been ratified by regular usage. Nor, as far as I can tell, has it ever been used to refer to a sequence that occurs within the individual, or that could take place during the reading of a novel, poem or any other literary creation. Certain critics speak of an aesthetic process, and also of a literary situation. The reason for putting "literary process" in inverted commas is to suggest a correlation between the psychoanalytical process, the dynamics of which I will explain presently, and the sequence of events that comprise the emotional and cognitive experience of the reader as they are impacted by a literary work.

DOI: 10.4324/9781003342472-3

2 A Sphere of Communication: the Analytical Situation

What we now call the analytical process was the decisive discovery of Freud, who found that when two people – the analyst and the patient – are in a certain communicative situation, the psychoanalytical situation, there occurs in the observable and immediate therapeutic space a fruitful, asymmetrical exchange which favours the dramatization of the patient's deepest, most inveterate structures. These structures, which have taken shape through the internalization of the lived past, become capable of internal figurative representation in the conscious and unconscious imagination. They may be transported or transferred outwards to another time, and to other relational spaces. One of these spaces is the psychoanalytical session, which is painstakingly prepared in such a way as to enable the best possible representation of this inner life or scenario; this inner theatre where our own self interacts with the images we have formed of others.

The analytical situation, with all the conditions in which the two protagonists find themselves, is a sphere of communication and, therefore, of interpersonal interaction. It is an intersection where the remote past and the most immediate present engage in dialogue, and where the analyst and patient together enact hitherto unspoken situations, indeed situations that have not previously been reflected upon. Similarly, they experience together emotions to which no verb or image had previously been attached, and which still await, in order to become conscious, an external support. In this case, this external support comes from the analyst and from the frame he provides, in which these situations and emotions can be reflected upon extensively enough to be articulated verbally and made thinkable and knowable.

The intersection of the analytical situation also enables the confluence of all kinds of emotions and impulses which populate precisely or obscurely the patient's psychic reality, which, in the clinical setting, have a unique opportunity to be, and to become. Dreams, phantasies, amorphous emotions, corporeal sensations and desires find, outside of the subject and in the concrete and present reality of the analyst, a configuration which makes them more relevant, more real. Further, whatever comes to the patient from the outside, in this case from the analyst, finds its meaning in the sediment of the patient's personal history.

2.1 Process or dead end

The communicative circle between the analyst and the patient, and between inside and outside; this continuous and simultaneous experience of affecting and being affected, is enhanced by its maximum development in the analytical session. When things go well, the relationship between patient and analyst in the session undergoes a more or less profound change, which is in fact part of the therapeutic or psychoanalytical process. In short, I would say that this change, often described as a realization, or as emotional maturation, follows from the gradual acquisition of self-knowledge or insight. It comprises an increasing differentiation of feelings and of the experience of oneself. It enables the lessening of adhesion to and confusion with others; others who gradually cease to function as part of the matrix of individual identity. Instead of merely echoing the projections of the less acknowledged aspects of the individual's psyche, objects acquire their own free and autonomous nature. Thus, the subject increasingly acknowledges these aspects, in an ongoing process of discovery, arising out of a progressive acceptance of one's solitude. Nevertheless, this is a solitude which results in the formation of more authentic connections; it is a solitude that is pregnant with creative potential, and which is a far cry from the alienating and claustrophobic atmosphere of the symbiotic relationship.

At the same time, this differentiation of self and other results in another kind of anxiety: instead of the fear of disintegration, depersonalization or inner incoherence, this new uneasiness has to do with the need to preserve a fruitful relationship with the object, despite the inevitable conflict that every bond entails. The subject must also accept, in fact, the conflict that arises out of the convergence of love and hate. In different kinds of relationship, he comes to trust his capacity for joy and pleasure, and his capacity to endure suffering; there is also an increasing sense of responsibility for the joy and suffering of others. Despite the growing potential for contact involving conflict, the subject is not overwhelmed, and can trust the adequacy of his own impulses. This confidence in a sufficiently robust unconscious frees him from the risk of being anxiously hypervigilant, characteristic of someone who lives in denial of everything that might trigger a state of anxiety.

All this could be summed up more succinctly by saying that the psychoanalytical process may lead to a more harmonious equilibrium in the development of the Oedipus complex: a complex because it involves an adequate harmonization of one's bisexuality, the pain resulting from a confused relationship with one's mother, the acceptance of the loss of the child's love objects, the prevailing identification with the parent of one's own sex, the ability to deal with envy and jealousy and to negotiate the inevitable ambivalence in one's amorous and sexual life.

So far we have been addressing only the best possible outcomes of the psychoanalytic process, but there are many other possible outcomes. Communication has its pitfalls, and though we can steer it towards a revelation of the unknown, and towards a knowledge or inner and outer reality, we will also encounter many obstacles on the path. And it must also be said that this full communicative potentiality is not always felt to be entirely desirable. Contact with reality and with truth generates anxiety. The change that a fuller knowledge enables and even requires can be experienced as catastrophic (Bion).

Fear of this catastrophic change leads many relationships to become routine and insipid, supported only by the repetition of that which is commonplace at the expense of anything new and progressive. Such fear, which can be seen in any type of relationship – amorous, ludic, professional and so on – can also characterize an analytical situation. In that case, instead of a therapeutic process, we are dealing with a dead end, or an *Impasse*.

Two people can meet in order to expand, in a communication exchange, the horizon of their respective possibilities, and they can do this ardently, with all the risks of the unforeseen. But they can also, either subtly or more candidly, agree to take refuge in many possible areas of contact. In the case of such a pact or conspiracy, there is a conscious or unconscious denial of the truth, and with it, a denial of hope and anxiety; it leads to all kinds of repression and dissociations. Instead of truth and knowledge, what is fomented is tranquillity at all costs, the ritualization of life, the more or less magical control of the unforeseeable; in a certain sense, error and deception. The particular technical conditions that the psychoanalyst creates are adequate to bring to the surface these impulses towards denial, this assault against bonding, and the sabotage that is inflicted on any possibility of reciprocal knowledge.

The path to which communication can lead is uncertain in any kind of human relationship. It then comes as no surprise that in the analyst–patient relationship, the vast array of expressive and receptive possibilities will generate, alongside the desire to clarify and understand one's own conflicts, a compulsive tendency to deny or diffuse them, particularly when live contact with anxiety that is thus revealed triggers unbearable discomfort.

The same could be said of other kinds of relationship, such as friendships or love relations, and also of group dynamics, with all their highs and lows of creative cooperation and neutral or self-destructive routine. If these fluctuations occur in all kinds of relational contexts, it is worth considering how they operate and evolve in the particular relationship between the text and the reader.

3 Another Sphere of Communication: the Literary Situation

The relationship between the author or text and the reader is also asymmetrical. The exchange is, in principle, unidirectional, flowing from the author to reader with no possibility of feedback, because in most cases the reader does not communicate directly with the author, or with the concrete reality of the author as a person. I say that because I want to discuss how a relationship with the author nonetheless takes place inwardly, in the reader's psychic reality, even very intensely. It is to this relationship and its vicissitudes that we assign the term "literary process". What I propose to do is look more closely at the particularities of the communicative relationship that is established between the author and reader, with reference to the relationship between analyst and patient.

On the basis of this hypothetical analogy, we might ask whether it is the author or the reader who plays the role of the analyst. We were discussing this recently with Meg Harris. Who is the analyst and who is being analysed? It is obvious that it is the author who does most of the speaking. The author describes the things that he sees and that affect him, and he expresses himself indirectly in his narration of a situation or description of a landscape, in the delineation of his characters and in the vicissitudes of their stories.

We can say then that in this exposition of himself and the world, a world that may be suffering or rejoicing, the author is offering himself to his audience in a way that is comparable to the way in which the patient offers himself, through what he says or through his silences, to the analyst in the here and now of the analytic situation. Similarly, the poet and the dramatist also display and conceal, actualize and at the same time obscure certain aspects of themselves, as they speak in the first, second, and third person.

3.1 The text and the reader

I have so far discussed just one aspect of the author–reader relationship. But the author's exposing, offering or describing himself, is only one very partial aspect of his communication to the reader. It presupposes a reader who is also reduced to a single possible dimension, the most appropriate name for which might be that of critic; a spectator almost more interested in who the author is than in what he has to say. It must be recognized that this is not the most usual or stable attitude exhibited by the reader. A literary work, perhaps especially if it is efficient and valid, makes us forget the author. It makes more sense to talk about a text–reader than an author–reader relationship. Faced with the description of a landscape, or with the twists and turns of a plot or with the vicissitudes of a character, the object we are dealing with, as readers, is not the author but the text. It is only afterwards, as we reflect upon the text, rather than when we are in full flow of the reading or the performance, that we consider the one who has offered us so many aspects of himself through his poem, drama or novel.

Perhaps it is only in the case of the poet, who writes while looking directly at us, all the time having in mind who will end up listening; or who scolds us from his wounded or joyful intimacy, that we as readers feel engaged by the subject who lives within the poetic image which, more or less, reveals him. Even so, even in this extreme case, despite the strident clarion calls, or apostrophizing, the individual writing forgoes any precise definition, and at the same time pours himself into the text. The poet, in his personal singularity, often eludes us while we read. Then, the object that we are truly dealing with is not the poet's precise external reality, but the condensed way in which it has been metaphorized in the text.

3.2 *The literary situation and its destination*

That said, while the text is our object, one which obscures and at the same time reveals the author who has produced it, it does have another primordial aspect and role. By that I mean that the text is a space, a sphere, a scenario that the author has constructed and set up, but has not fully populated. He has only constructed the scenic framework and placed there some objects and characters, which despite their precision are apt to combine with the different landscapes and characters that populate our own phantasies, where they will acquire their meaning and further form the setting, the situation, and the plot itself.

Thus, this space, the literary work, which is the meeting point between the author and reader, has for both parties certain features which I would say are entirely amphibious. On the one hand, the text is animated by the most intimate experience; on the other hand, it has external dimensions, and is limited by space and time, sounds and cadences. The sphere of the poem or novel is an intermediate region, which in psychoanalysis we refer to as transitional: transitional between subject and object, between inner and outer, where outer and inner converge and interact reciprocally. And it seems to me that this is as true for the author as for the reader. The poet dresses their affections, emotions, and conflicts in words which he selects from the broad and yet precise nominative repertoire of external objects. Lacking vocabulary to denote internal phenomena, he resorts to concrete representations of objects in the external world. Whether suddenly or little by little, the most intimate realities: an unnamed pleasure or an as yet undefined nostalgia or an impatience, experiences which are only felt vaguely and are impelled in a direction which remains imprecise, in an amorphous awareness of a strange rhythm or corporeal tension, find a space and a profile because they have been hosted by a fantasy in a three-dimensional image, in a scenario of movements and shapes. Now the still amorphous content of the mind has found a host which can accommodate it, and where it can acquire content and precision.

This meeting-point between the content and the container of it, can be multifaceted. When it is established with optimal correspondence, and with sufficient differentiation, there results what we call symbolic formation. The good author, or poet, is one who draws deeply from his emotional resources and finds, outside himself, the best possible outer attire for his inner world, the most fitting external objects, which may be words, verbal images and sequences of metaphors.

3.2.1 Insight. *Literary process*

These priceless symbolic constructions, which are interwoven as the text unfolds, possess for the author an amphibious quality, in that they are both internal and external at the same time. And yet, in their manifest verbal reality, arrayed as they are by the author, they constitute an external object that is susceptible to a vast range of interpretations by future readers, be they few or many. These readers, in order to actualize their feelings as a precise experience, have required an external host to accommodate them. When this occurs, we can refer to reading as a provider of insight, and to a literary process. The service the poet or dramatist renders to the reader is to make available to him sufficiently fertile external hosts to enable him to articulate the ineffable. The reader may have experienced and felt something inwardly, but had needed an external form such as a poem or certain aspects of it, an image or symbolic sequence, to help him reconfigure his inner world, to make the unthinkable thinkable, and give a durable shape to his deeply embedded amorphous magma of emotions which had needed words in order to fully exist, expand and cohere.

Thus, the literary creator, by offering this transitional sphere that is his creation, plays the role of therapist. It is a very substantial role as helper, in the sense that the literary creator enables us to recognize ourselves more fully by showing us what we are and what we are feeling.

But is this whole process all that distant and different from what happens during a psychoanalytical process? While it is obviously the case that in an analysis, analyst and patient do not literally produce poetry, nor any kind of literary text, the analytical process does have features in common with the literary process. In short, psychoanalysis is the setting for transformation of the unconscious, prompted by a communicative interaction.

It should be said that what psychoanalysis has contributed that is genuinely new is not the discovery of the unconscious. The unconscious, as has often been recognized, had already been discovered by others who were seriously committed to confronting the mystery of the self. Freud was by no means the first to speak about the unconscious, nor the first to refer to psychoanalysis. In fact, it was Coleridge who first used the term psychoanalysis. But it was Freud, with innovative geniality, who developed the psychoanalytical method, enabling a process wherein embryonic and partial forms of consciousness could become integrated into the texture of adult consciousness. It is precisely because of Freud's innovation that we can talk about the analogies between literary process and the process which unfolds in the consulting room. The psychoanalytical process has elements in common with the ardent gestation of contact with and articulation of deep emotional states that the author performs alone, initially, in the intimate experiences which will constitute the womb of the poem or novel they will end up creating. That said, when the poet writes or articulates his poem in silence, he is already playing a transitive therapeutic role. What begins as an inner, inescapable and even compulsive demand, has acquired another dimension: what the poet has been able to say about himself has already become a dialogue. The word is offered as a host for the doubts and anxieties of the readers who will later come to it. By this I do not mean that this therapeutic function of the poem was what prompted the poet to write it. This is rather a by-product of the literary creation. However, it becomes central in the author–reader dialogue, and in the emergence of the literary process.

We thus separate out the process taking place between the text and the reader from a previous process, undoubtedly intrapsychic, that moves the author to create. When I say that the poet, for example, tries to give shape to what is taking place in the deepest recesses of his emotional life, I also think that this occurs in the relationship that he is able to engender within himself, between himself and his internal objects; in other words, amidst the unconscious and conscious images he has of other people and things.

I also mean that the space where the session takes place, the context of the transference and the structures which support and sustain it, are in a sense comparable to a literary work. With the silence and the speech of the analyst, with the indefinite constancy of his presence that allows the patient to come into being, and to speak, a web of meanings is woven and dramatized with two actors, the analyst and the patient. This then gives flesh to all the characters of the patient's inner story, expressed through gesture, dream or discourse, all of which converge on the reality of being present and of their continued mutual affection.

Taking into account this dichotomy of the literary process, that is to say, the process that occurs in the internal world of the author which finds expression in the production of a text and, in addition, the one that unfolds in the minds of the possible readers in the particular way in which they are affected by the text, we understand the expressions of detachment on the part of many a poet or novelist with regard to their work.

They often consider it an entity with a life of its own which no longer belongs to them, which must follow its own unforeseeable course, with many possible destinations depending on the readers that it finds. The author partly disengages, showing no sign of either modesty or vanity, from what has so deeply been part of himself throughout the vicissitudes of the creative process.

In that, as we suggest, the author's work has brought about an authentic clarification of his conflicts, and has constituted a search for how to reflect these conflicts in a text, it also serves to precipitate an evolution in the author's own self-understanding. It is not only about the pleasure of representing himself in a text that the author seeks, because that is only the case with minor creations which are a form of recreation. Even in the case of a simple figurative itch, we cannot be certain that it lacks transcendence. However, when we resort to the external world to project ourselves, the objects we choose, and much less if they are people, are not so docile as to serve as faithful mirrors to what we project onto them. Undoubtedly, we take on the colour of these objects too; the physiognomy of the other, and there is a price to pay. The image that we pick up of ourselves as reflected in these external objects, comes back to us with other nuances and connotations.

When this occurs not as a form of recreation, or as a means of deriving pleasure, but rather as a search; as a penetrating enquiry into the unknown prompted by something deep within us, the experience does not end without our being transformed by it. In this transformation, our anxieties change, they are partially resolved and give us access to other perspectives. This might explain the notable disinterest on the part of the author in his own work once it is finished. When this occurs, the author is already an "other", and the work is a testimony to something that was extremely relevant, but which has now been left behind precisely because it was successful. It has enabled the author to move on in the never-ending process of his individuation.

This evolution of identity, of the self, is presented to us in the very content of a literary work. The destiny of the characters of a novel or drama develops in the course of the text, and reflects the fluctuations that occur in the mind of the author. His is a mind that functions, perhaps, as a "multiple personality": a personality which enters into crisis when the "personalities" or different parts of him collide with each other and show themselves to the greatest possible degree in order to be able to concur, or initiate a new, more promising, coexistence, or at least one that entails less suffering. And this does not happen only in the conception of a novel or play. The poet can also find verification by recourse to a type of elaborative dramatic technique. An example of this is the way in which Carles Riba describes the effort involved in the elaboration of a poem. This is literally what he says in the prologue of *Esbós de tres oratoris*: "More than once I have felt as if I were looking down on a theatre, in which I myself was multiplied in many persons: those that confronted each other on centre stage or those who were only present on the margins; I was all of them, each one in their own moment, and at the same time I was the one who was called to impose order on the confusion, as everyone was calling me the poet".

3.2.2 Disruptions in the literary process: acting out, collusions between the author and reader

The author–text–reader relationship, like all communications and acquisitions of knowledge, has its accidents and deficiencies. Here also we see a parallel with the fluctuations of the psychoanalytical process.

The reasons why the literary process can fail to get started, can make very slow progress, or even peter out in an *impasse* and finally in a rupture between the text and the reader, are many and varied. In some cases the foregoing are attributable to the particularities of the text, but they are also always related to the reader's willingness to go on engaging with the text. For example, the text might induce too much anxiety, or not enough. It might encourage the denial of all conflict, having a great deal in common with the defence mechanisms that we encounter in an analytic session and which obstruct the therapeutic process. In other cases, the text presents itself openly as a kind of manic triumph over the very idea of conflict, which it ridicules and lambasts, more or less insolently, but also with wit, sarcasm or black humour.

But in all these occurrences, what matters most, as I have said, is the reader's particular receptivity. This means that the same text can for some be a source of anxiety, and for others, a tranquilizing influence. It is very difficult to speak of terror-inducing texts, moralizing texts, or depressing texts; terror, moral norm or sadness are emotions which can only be understood in relational contexts and therefore depend on the connection that is established between subject and object.

We can also say that what the text offers us might be a far cry from the acquisition of insight, or the gaining of any penetrating knowledge concerning oneself. There are texts with an essentially ludic purpose, and while it is true that any pastime or recreation can make us feel renewed, a text whose aim is to amuse us can actually serve to create an evasive parenthesis rather than connect us with our intimate reality. In such cases, a text can be somewhat perverse, in the sense that it offers opportunities to mystify the truth, thus allowing us to deny the emergence of any conflict in our conscious mind.

This range of possibilities that the text offers may have multitudinous effects, including the incitation to identify with the characters we meet in the story, or with the author himself. Where do we position ourselves as readers? Do we identify with one or other of the characters, or with the author who has created them? In the dramatic action of the narrative, and in particular as spectators of theatre plays or films, it is not hard to become aware of the options; of the identificatory choices that we make which lead us away from the seat in which we are sitting into the skin of one or other of the characters. It is also important to reflect on the stable or volatile quality of our choice. Sometimes the identification is so intense that it does not end when we leave the theatre. After the performance we continue to behave to a lesser or greater extent like this or that protagonist: such as Captain Thunder or Tintin, in the case of children, or as Antigone or Don Juan, in the case of adults. Thus, unaware of our disguise, we are still living a somewhat eccentric life; that is to say, one that is located outside ourselves. We all know how far this confusion can take us beyond the transitional space of the period of reading, or of the performance. Suddenly, the book and the stage lose their frame and we continue to act outside of them, in the other settings of our lives. Here the term acting out becomes relevant.

We know that these confusions, born of an emotionally rich relationship with the text, can be tragic, as has been the case with some readers of Werther; or picturesque, as with the existentialist fashions in Sartre's post-war Paris; or they can be tender, as in the mass enthusiasm with which New Yorkers congregated on the docks to wait for the ships that would bring the latest chapters of the stories Dickens was writing in London. We learn from Malcolm Andrew's report in the prologue of *The Old Curiosity Shop*, that on one such occasion, the latest chapters of this work were awaited with great impatience; the crowds gathered wondering about the vicissitudes of the characters. Perhaps anticipating this restlessness, the captain of the vessel, just about to dock, stepped out onto the deck and shouted through a megaphone, "Little Nell is dead!" It is well-known that the sentimentality and tearful atmosphere of certain passages in the book drew criticism, some of it sarcastic. For example, Oscar Wilde famously said that it takes a heart of stone to read about the death of Little Nell without laughing.

Yet without stepping outside during the course of the reading itself, we remain identified with one or other character, whilst the author presses him or her to limits that would be unbearable for us. There comes a time when the identification becomes uncomfortable, and the reader feels imprisoned within the character. Then the identification must be abandoned, or at least endured with much less agreement.

At other times, the reading or performance invites us to switch identifications, as if in doing so we could "taste", so to speak, the experience of more than one of the characters. When we do this, we are beginning to identify with the author, who in fact projects himself into all of his characters, albeit with different degrees of preference. Such identification with the author also means that what happens on stage or screen can line up with what is happening in our psychic reality, in the sense that in our internal theatre, parts of us bond, collide or disconnect with external characters, depending on the situations we find ourselves in.

Thus, a large part of the repertoire of attitudes on the part of the patient vis-à-vis the analyst can also be found in the particular setting of the act of reading. To complete the analogy, we could also mention the separation anxiety we might experience when we forget the contents of a book, or lose it, or flick through the penultimate pages. We could also mention the times when we give up reading in the earliest pages of a novel, which is perhaps comparable to interrupting the therapy in its early stages, or at more or less critical moments, when it becomes intolerable, for whatever reason, to proceed. In all these cases, where suffering cannot be endured, there is an *acting out*. That is to say, instead of an elaboration of the conflict in the fantasy that the author creates and presents to us, the conflict is dramatized outwardly, more or less abruptly. What is dramatized on the stage of daily reality are the emotions that cannot be contained in the secluded atmosphere of the reading session.

4 The Analyst Analysed

We have suggested that in the literary situation the roles played by the author and the reader are in some sense interchangeable. In maintaining that the author and his text can trigger changes in the reader, so, assuming a parallelism between literary and analytical situations, the author has assumed the role of analyst. In fact, through his text he has catalysed or mobilized within the reader of all kinds of reactions: from the opening of new horizons of feeling and thought, to the short-circuiting or rupturing of such reactions.

That said, these attitudes and responses on the part of the reader to the "analyst-author" are reversed when, due to some emotional reaction that the reading prompts, the reader leaves the scenario created by the text, ends his identification with, or sympathies or antipathies towards the characters, and begins to think about and focus on the author instead. It is comparable to a spell being broken; we leave the setting established by the text, but not in order simply to act out in other realities. No. In fact, as readers, we remain very close to the setting, but it is as if it had lost its substance, its tangible materiality, to become a transparent or opaque window through which to discern the mind of the author. The roles are reversed. Now the reader, assuming the role of critic, has become the analyst. And the author is now the analysed analyst.

I would say that the analysis being practised in this case on the part of the reader as casual or professional critic is more inquisitive than that which takes place when the author is playing the part of analyst. In fact, the author could tell us that the reader was not subjecting the author to analysis at all, but was rather engaging with the author's memory of his own self-analysis, a self-analysis that was subtly occupying the reader's mind. The reader, through his reactions and through what he perceived or did not perceive in the text, or through that which pleased him or made him suffer, was entering more and more into the experience of being a patient. But this was happening allegorically through a third mediating object, the text, with the freedom that is afforded when we are able to pick up the text or put it down, despite its hold on us and the seductive power that it has to retain our attention during and after the reading session.

By contrast, when the reader or critic turns this situation around, everything is different. The analysed author has less freedom to escape. He has left his personal mark very precisely on the text, and however discontent he is with this fact, the author remains available to be subjected entirely to the reader's analysis. The content and style of his work, with all its connotations regarding his personal life and his literary and biographical past, is available for scrutiny.

The reader-critic, as analyst, is much more incisive and interrogating than the author. At certain times, literary theory has led to what, in our field, we refer to as a wild analysis, an analysis essentially of contents. That is to say, it has tended to see the text as a symptom of the author; a symptom which might mask or hint at some feature or other of his unconscious mind. Fortunately, however, the reader-critic who passes from being the patient to playing the part of analyst, has also evolved, as have psychoanalytical technique and theory. Now we no longer practise the type of psychoanalysis that considered the mind of the patient as an object to be painstakingly dissected. That was a relic of a medical model that was more suited to the reality of objects in nature than to human nature, even when corporeal reality is involved.

Analysing a symptom, a dream or a gesture, is not something that can be approached as if it were a foreign body. Now we cannot conceive of the study of any aspect of human behaviour without considering it in the context of a relationship and a history, and, more precisely, of the relationship that the patient has with the analyst while therapy is under way.

I suggest that literary criticism, which I would venture to think has been influenced by psychoanalysis, or perhaps has simply evolved autochthonously, has developed in the same direction. That is to say, by placing emphasis not only on the biography or unconscious intentions of the author, but, especially, on the conscious and unconscious affinity that the author has created with the reader through the medium of the text.

5 Psychoanalytical Process, Literary Process, and Transference

The literary process, when it is managed beneficially, has quite a well-defined trajectory. It begins with a centrifugal movement in which the reader is transported, or, if you prefer, transfers the images of his or her inner world that are awakened by the text, into the sphere that is created through reading. This is a space of a mixed nature where parts of the reader and the external reality of the poem or drama meet. The atmosphere created is a kind of twilight, which illuminates things with external clarity and inner radiance: two lights which graft the splendour of the past onto the clarity of the present. But the reader is not lost in this territory where, without knowing it, part of his internal drama is being played out. He is not lost. In fact, the experience that the text gives him is not a delirious one, even though the reader may momentarily feel that he has lost his mind. While a text takes us, strictly speaking, out of ourselves, it also allows us to return to our central home with a fresh store. Even if, for a more or less prolonged moment we have remained in this twilight zone between inner and outer; if we have taken up residence, as Rilke puts it, between daytime and the dream, we nevertheless return with a renewed ability to make contact with others and with objects. The objects of the text had been our hosts when in our centrifugal movement we had immersed ourselves in them; now we are their host and we press them into the inveterate moulds of our memories. This return to ourselves is unpredictable, because it depends on our particular state of mind during the moment of return. This will determine whether our entry into the universe the author invites us into will be rough or smooth. But there are unmistakeable signs of this beginning. It is that moment that another poet, this time a contemporary one, beautifully defines in one of his essays. I am referring to Yves Bonnefoy, who mentions the point at which we interrupt our reading, when we lift our eyes from our book and allow in the atmosphere evoked in it, where we have been living with a greater or lesser degree of plenitude. It is the moment when the meaning of the text can begin to acquire value for us; that is to say, when it reanimates images and words from our own memories or present experiences. And Bonnefoy gives us an example: "How can we read, 'forgotten woods where the winter penetrates', without entering woods of our own, to live in them for a while, and get lost in them?"

This reflection by the poet will serve to shed light on the phenomenon of transference in the reading situation, and, I would say, highlights its central role in the so-called literary process. As critics and readers, we can report the experience of this circular process of projection of our intimacy onto the screen of the text and of "reintrojection"; the recovery of ourselves, and the integration of that which has affected us and which is changing us. It is clear that I am describing here a frankly successful literary process, whose effectiveness lies in the abundance and quality of everything that the text was able to mobilize and extract from us, in this outpouring of our inner world when projected onto the drama or poem.

However, as I have pointed out before, everything could end there, in alienation without an introjective return, such as when this transference is perpetuated without becoming conscious. We already know what this leads to. It is to a mimetic disguise where the text takes hold of us, and mimics our own postural or verbal habits, or makes us adopt in a more general way the behaviour and habits of one or other of the characters. We can be docilely receptive to the text's ideology, to its décor or sexual atmosphere, for example. This can range from harmless mimicry to suicide: the irresolute transference of the literary situation offers many variations on the same basic condition: a condition which entails confusion in trapping the reader in this oneiric web that the text has spun, and from which he has not been able to disentangle himself.

But while the process does not end with this first projective movement, and the immersion of ourselves in the text does not embed us in an excentric experience, but rather allows us to connect us with a new source of light, it does involve a certain reconfiguration of ourselves, affected and changed as we are through the emotional experience that contact with the literary work has induced.

There is a difference in the way that this process begins in the case of drama or novels as compared with poetry. In drama and in the novel, the author lets us see quite clearly how he is going about his task. His characters, which represent their inner world in conflict, have to reorganize themselves. Or rather the author's conflicts require personification to instantiate the forces struggling within them. The result is the same. The author, to express his conflicts, seeks out characters capable of embodying them, or such characters are already clearly delineated in the fantasy, and call on the author to organize them sequentially, thus enabling them to interact and find resolution. Pirandello referred to characters in search of an author. But at the same time, he, like every other author, also shows how he needs characters to express what moves him to joy or anguish.

In the analytical situation, the text is provided by the patient, but the sphere in which it becomes dramatic material is the psychoanalytical technique and the way in which the analysis is framed. This framing, with its particular conditions of utterance and listening, is what facilitates the transit from corporeal feelings, mental states and phantasy to shouts, gestures, and words. There is a script which precedes and at the same time gives shape to the dramatic action of the session, and there is the analyst who plays the role of narrator, who explains what is happening or what has just happened between himself and the patient ... And there follows an explanation in two voices of why it happened at that particular moment, and of how the framing and the attitude of the analyst invoked that particular script and, with it, the imaginary characters who, in the patient's inner world, live in silence, or in whichever other way, in the scenarios of his everyday reality.

This dramatization on the transference stage, as Meltzer neatly expressed it, does have an element of theatrical arrangement, but also a certain kind of poetic organization. Without these particular poetic ingredients, the representation would not be complete. One essential prerequisite is the creation of an imprecise, but sufficiently and optimally supervised, atmosphere comprising past and present, love and hatred, and also truth and fiction. This is the transference atmosphere in which the analyst and the patient make contact, this territory belonging to no one, and to everyone, in which the latent experiences of the patient are played out and represented, and where the dramatic to-and-fro of discursive reconsideration finds clarification.

Despite these analogies and coincidences, I want not to omit to mention the differences and contrasts between the analytical and literary situations. The poet's ambiguity is reflected in the particular way he makes use of language, or searches for a word which he works over and weighs up, and with which he can represent what is most imprecise and diffuse about himself, and what he is able to avoid telling us (as Bonnefoy reminds us). By contrast, in the analytical situation, ambiguity entails a tension which permeates every detail of the interaction between patient and analyst. Everything that passes between them is a little antagonistic or paradoxical: precision regarding the time of the session, the schedule, and the imprecision of the subject-matter which is subject to the randomness of a carefully cultivated spontaneity; the proximity of the analyst in the chair, with the patient on the couch, both of whom nevertheless avoid the reciprocal impact of eye-contact and body language; the cultivated freedom of verbal expression and the reduction of this expression to a relationship which is held in suspense outside the time limits of the session, and the fact that the patient knows nothing of the private life of the analyst ... All this conspires to create the oneiric atmosphere I was referring to earlier, where conscious and unconscious converge, where a phantasy can be embodied and articulated and may give rise to a dramatic sequence on the stage that is the therapy session.

I will return now, by way of conclusion, to this space where the analytical process takes place. It is within this space that the reflections I have tried to elucidate have taken shape. These reflections have led me to consider *transference as a phenomenon that is common and central both to the analytical situation and to the literary one*: central and indeed indispensable for initiating a process of change in either the patient or the reader.

I have tried to spell out the fact that while the phenomenon of transference is basically the same in its different manifestations, the reason for this is that it concerns such elemental psychic activities as the capacity for perception and symbolic function. It is therefore no surprise that transference can be found in a range of different settings. Neither is it surprising that Freud chose the polysemic term *Übertragung* to denote such a generic phenomenon, a term which, in modern German means to transport, translate or contaminate, or to transfer money from one account to another, etc. By situating this concept at the core of the analytical situation, this transport, this traffic, can be made to apply to all kinds of psychic activities: the transposition or transference of impulses, feelings, images, and intimate and unconscious situations. All such psychic activity, though in some sense temporally remote, takes shape in the interpersonal present of the relationship with the analyst in the here and now of the analytic session.

That said, as I have perhaps insisted too much, whilst the phenomenon of transference is generic and common to both the psychoanalytical and literary situations, the means by which it manifests are very different and specific. In psychoanalysis, everything is set up so as to make the transference as obvious and conscious as possible. When this aim is fully realized, the possibility of play, and of representation, may be recognized by the patient. As such, there is the real possibility of meeting in this intermediate space created by the analyst, to which Freud conferred the entire analytical function in his essay *Remembering, Repeating and Working Through*, 1914. This awareness of the ludic element, of the figurative exercise of phantasy, is, as Meredith Skura points out, the beginning of symbolic construction, which is a primary version of art.

I will conclude by exemplifying, through a brief clinical anecdote, the effort made by an 11-year-old girl, in a situation in which it was particularly challenging emotionally to recognize, in the midst of her present reality and her acute suffering, this intermediate and symbolic setting which she and I were building together in the course of a long treatment process.

This girl, who suffered with severe depersonalization anxieties, was living with a psychotic father. This, together with the comfort she found in being welcomed into an intensive therapeutic process which she doubtless idealized, gave her communication a depth, virtually adult-like, that is rarely encountered in a patient of that age.

The session that I am referring to, the last one of the week, was very painful, not only because the girl had to deal with living with her psychotic father at a time when her mother had just left. Under these circumstances, I was experienced as the mother who left her when she most needed her and also as the unpredictable and seductive father.

Towards the end of the session, the girl remembers that her mother showed concern for her father, but not for her. When she had scarlet fever, for example, she said: "She only stayed with me one night ..." Jealousy comes to the forefront and her tone becomes resentful and embittered. Suddenly, she asks me, "And what do you do on Sundays?" A little taken aback, I reacted by saying that it was obvious that I wasn't with her, and that she knew I was with others, as her mother was with her father.

Her first reaction was a contained tension, before this turned into open contempt ... After a short silence she said to me, "Look, I couldn't care less about my parents ... They are pointless ... and don't start going on about when I was little ... I wanted to be born, and so I was born". After saying that she ignored me and started to play with the toy cars on the table. But her play didn't hold her attention for long and she lost interest. Then she said to me, "I wish there were no cars, just bicycles, like mine. Cars are all stupid".

It was clear to me that cars for her represented adults, including me. In a way that turned out to be unfortunate, I said to her, "All cars are stupid? Even if you could drive?" I wanted to comment on her indignation towards me, who represented these adults and these parents who had neglected her, now that we were about to break until Monday. She only half-heard me, because she started to shout, "They are all stupid, I can't stand them, I can't stand them!"

I had the feeling that I had turned on a tap, that I had opened the floodgates of her rage by hinting at her weakness as a bicycle-child in the face of the arbitrariness of adults. There was a long silence, during which time she started to play with the toy cars again ... She rearranged them on the table, but then lost interest again, and she did not manage to organize her play in any kind of sequence. She seemed turned in on herself, and her expression became unfocused ...

Eventually, she turned towards me and said, "I would like to know what it's like to die and then come back to life again. I think I'm dreaming, and that dying is waking up again ... Now I'm dreaming that I'm coming here". Her tone is very serious, vacillating, with an interrogating look in her eyes. Then I said to her, "When you are angry because hunger hurts you inside – she had mentioned her hunger at the start of the session – and you feel empty, and I'm with someone else, like your parents when they aren't with you ... Do you see what's happening? Your parents are not really parents anymore, it is you that has given yourself the desire to be born". The child interrupted me with a smile and said, "yes of course, of course! –, and I also vanish into thin air, I'm just a shadow, someone in one of your dreams".

The girl, towards the end of this interpretation, becomes restless and practically shouts out, "No, no, no you aren't just a shadow, no way, you are very real ... it's just that you are dreaming too. Yes, yes, we have met, really met, during our dream ..."

I think this could be characterized as transference in the analytical situation, as a sphere of multiple encounters – of outer and inner, past and present, love and hate, in a setting made available so that the dreams and phantasies of the patient might acquire volume and speech, and might surpass themselves through the resonance and extension they find in the mind of the analyst. The analyst then, in his cognitive capacity and in his phantasy, formulates these into an interpretation. And all of this is held in a present continuous at the very border of action, but without crossing it. This would constitute for me a clinical description of transference, and within it, the construction of the symbol, both of which are basic common elements in the psychoanalytical and literary situations.

Note

1 First published in *Psicoanàlisi i Literatura* (Fundació Caixa Pensions, De set a nou. n. 31). Barcelona, 1990.

Bibliography

Andrew, M. (1949) Introduction, in Charles Dickens, *The Old Curiosity Shop*, Penguin Books, London.
Bion, W. R. (1970) *Attention and Interpretation*, Tavistock Publications, London.
Bonnefoy, Y. (1988) Lever les yeux de son livre, *Nouvelle revue de psychanalyse*, no. 37.
Freud, S. (1914) *Erinnern, Wiederholden und Durcharbeiten. Ges. Werke-Imago*, 1949.
Freud, S. (1916) *Introducció a la Psicoanàlisi*, Edicions 62, Barcelona, 1986.
Meltzer, D. (1967) *The Psycho-Analytical Process*, Heinemann, London.
Meltzer, D. (1983) *Dream-Life*, Clunie Press.
Riba, C. (1957) Esbós de tres oratoris (pròleg), in *Obres Completes* I, Edicions 62, Barcelona, 1965.
Skura, M. A. (1981) *The Literary Use of the Psychoanalytic Process*, Yale University Press, New Haven CT and London.

4 *Symbolon* and *Diabolon* in the Transference[1]

Pere Folch Mateu

1 Lexical Considerations

In order to aid understanding of what I shall be discussing here, a brief linguistic clarification about the symbol and transference is in order.

The word "symbol" comes from the Greek word *symbolon*, the noun corresponding to the verb *symballo*, which means to throw or put together. The verb is composed of *-ballo* (which means to throw) and the prefix *sym-* (signalling togetherness or participation), which we find in words like sympathy and symposium (originally, drink in company). An equivalent prefix *co-*, is found in words like com-passion and co-operation.

A symbol, then, represents the bringing together, or approximation of, things that were once at a distance. It is the meeting point of things that were once far from each other. This happened in a very concrete way when, in ancient Greece, two people from the same sect or group recognized each other by fitting together two halves of a broken object. The once broken, whole object was then a password that made it possible to come in through an entrance. The anecdote is, in itself, symbolic. It indicates, as Laplanche and Pontalis point out, that sense is made by putting into relation what was once separate. It was with the *symbolon*, the sign thus reconstructed, that the Greeks could enter the temple or the fortress. It is also thanks to the symbol, which is to say the link that endows sense, that we can enter into knowledge of *the non-apparent, the ineffable, and, as psychoanalysts, the unconscious.*

Yet there is another Greek word of special interest, namely the antonym of *symbolon*, the word *diabolon*. In this term, the verb *ballo* (to throw) has the same meaning. The reverse sense comes from *dia-* which, contrary to the prefix *sym-*, has the opposite meaning to approximation. We find it in such English words as discord, diaspora, diastole, and so on. What these words all share is the sense of distance, widening, and separation. *Diabolon* would therefore mean to throw into the distance or to separate. As Jaume Medina recalls, the devil, the diabolical, is the one who separates, uncouples and dissociates. It is the Greek version of the Hebrew word *śāṭān* (to plot against), which means two things: devil and adversary.

DOI: 10.4324/9781003342472-4

Then again, *transfer* is, as we know, a word containing a prepositional prefix, *trans-*, plus *fer*, deriving from the Latin verb *ferre*, which means to carry or to bear. The verb can be joined with different prefixes, giving words like prefer, refer, and transfer which would suggest carrying forward, back, or there, respectively. This notion of carrying is found in other verbs like *translate*, which contains the past participle form of the verb *ferre*, which is *latus* (meaning borne or carried), so it implies taking from one place to another, or carrying from one language to another. This bearing, or carrying from one language to another has yet another lexical expression in the word *metaphor*. It sounds very different from transfer, transport, and translate because, instead of having a Latin origin, it comes from the Greek *metaphora* where its parts *meta* and *pherein* mean "over" and "carry" or "bear", respectively, so it literally signals a carrying over.

When Freud wanted to name the process which appeared in clinical work, which he saw as a kind of carrying from one place to another, he used the German term *Übertragung*, which translates as transmission or transference. It describes a transporting of the drives and of the emotions experienced in childhood to the present of the analytical situation; a carrying over of the longings and desires felt in the relationship with the mother and father, into the relationship with the analyst.

2 Direction and Content of the Transference

At the clinical level, we often wonder about what is transported, what is moved from one place to another, and from where. We wonder what the starting point and destination of the transference is. Perhaps the second question is easier to answer. We shall begin with that question and answer it with the help of a clinical vignette.

A patient begins a session in one of the early weeks of his psycho-analytic treatment, by saying that he doesn't understand why psycho-analysts give such importance to anxiety. He remarks, "I don't know what this is, and if I have ever noted any unease, it's not difficult to make it go away ... Yes, sometimes when I'm alone and the only thing I can do is mull over things, I start worrying ... For example, when I'm driving the car, then the thing's very simple. I speed up, step on the accelerator, and I don't feel anxious anymore. Well, yes, I'm very attentive and, if I'm going around the city, I focus on one street and the next one, on what might be coming at me from every corner ... I'd like to know what you're going to say about that ..."

In this brief passage, the patient speaks of different forms of transportation or transferences. First, he tells us that something he has experienced as disturbing has gone from inside to outside. When he steps on the accelerator, every concern, anxiety, or danger in which he might experience his worry is transported to the dangers of traffic, represented by the car that could come at him from a corner. With the "traffic" from inside to outside, the patient's worry has changed. According to him, he had something vaguely bothering him in his imagination, a sense of disquiet that wasn't clear – half fantasy, half bodily discomfort – but after he accelerated everything acquired clarity, the danger wasn't vague, but could appear in the form of a truck or motorbike at any corner. Something had been transposed from inside to outside, from his body to a specific place on the street, from the preconscious mists of a bad memory to the clear representation of a car crashing into him.

The patient kept moving between certain subjects, talking and talking about his work at the hospital and at home, and the holiday rota. His speech was so rigorous and nonstop that I couldn't find a way to intervene and point out to him the hurtling pace the session was acquiring. Finally, when I did manage to speak, he firmly interrupted me, telling me that just then something had occurred to him and that this could explain what he'd been saying up to that point. The patient had clearly felt my intervention as a crash into him, a disagreeable surprise that should have been foreseen and evaded. The situation of analysis awakened in him experiences or phantasies of being invaded, of being subject to the intrusive behaviour of others. His fear of being invaded, and also of criticism and punishment, mobilized phantasies of expulsion, of getting rid of things that troubled him. In the most concrete sense, this was related with the anal mode of expulsion.

However, the aim now is not to present particular knowledge of a clinical case but to consider the question about the points of departure and arrival of this transporting or transferring. The most evident kind of transport in the session fragment above is, as I have said, from inside to outside. At the same time, another kind of transport is evident: from bodily discomfort and disquiet to an accelerated narrative. What was concrete in feeling has become verbal. Discomfort, unease, and worry in relation to an internal object has become a specific relationship with an external object: the risk of traffic. All of this is quite conscious and observable by the patient himself. However what is not so conscious – or at least wasn't in this session at an early stage of his treatment – is the intolerable quality of the musings and self-recriminations which, if he wasn't careful, the patient imposed upon himself despite their apparent absurdity. This other transit, supposedly from an unconscious phantasy to a conscious state of unease, bodily discomfort and fretting, corresponds to Freud's first account of transference (*The Interpretation of Dreams*, 1900, chapter 7). Here, transference is described as the vehicle by which unconscious content that is loaded with affect, is moved to consciousness. It is a content that must be camouflaged before censorious eyes, hidden behind some banal appearance or more neutral guise. In our example, the experience of an object that gnaws inside becomes the threat of a vehicle that could crash into the patient. The patient had also recognized that recriminations from his head of department, and at other times from his parents, had stayed inside him and filled him with rancour. We could therefore answer the second question by saying that the itinerary of the transfer goes from inside to outside, from concrete to verbal, from unconscious to conscious, from past to present.

It should be noted that at the start of any treatment, our presumptions are mere inferences that may be contradicted or confirmed only in subsequent sessions, sometimes weeks or months later. Hence, the patient may tell us in the initial interviews about important aspects of his life: the atmosphere of his childhood, the characters of his parents, and about the people of his present milieu. This description is naturally his own, subjective view, which reflects the way he has more or less faithfully, or indeed with great distortion, internalized his dealings with others. Every patient and all of us represent ourselves to ourselves. We have constructed a version of our story and it is this, so to say, personal myth that counts in our present life. This story, in one way or another, is then transported or transferred to present experiences. For my patient, the construction he made of his father was of quite a bitter, pernickety man who wanted to impose his views and who, "showed you up even for the slightest carelessness". From the little we know at the time of the session I have reported, we can infer that this internalized father, as a superego function, attacked the patient from within. It seems this internal father obliged my patient to deal with this representation of father in just the way he had dealt with his external father when they were cohabiting during the patient's adolescence. At that time, the patient ducked the issue, disregarded things, or argued interminably with his father. We could say then that the transference goes from the internal object to the external object; from the father to the driver of the car that might eventually crash into my patient.

However, there is yet another kind of transport that appears in the session, of which the patient was fairly, but not wholly, ignorant. It is a transport from the relationship with the internalized father to the relationship with the analyst. What the analytical situation revealed in this session was the possibility of being observed and perhaps criticized or blamed by somebody, the analyst, who could potentially be experienced as an intruder into the patient's psychic intimacy and who could, from that place, make the patient terribly uneasy and oblige him to think about all sorts of things. We see that in the here-and-now of the session the patient mobilizes an unconscious or pre-conscious internal situation that is expressed in his fear of being made uneasy by rumination which must be banished fast, through being situated in the risks and threats of traffic.

Yet this transport from the unconscious, the internal, to a specific, conscious external reality is not easily identifiable. The supposed unconscious phantasy is always an inference, if in fact a most necessary inference for giving sense to and an explanation for what happens in the session. Nonetheless, what is striking is that scenarios at each end of the transference chain arouse anxiety. At one end, the analyst–analysand situation awakens unease in the patient and, at the other end, so does his being on the lookout for frightening things that might happen in the street. It should be remembered that the unconscious isn't only to be found in the depths of psychic reality with a father recriminating his son from inside, or in the childhood experience of terror, half psychic, half bodily, that must be evacuated with faeces, or in the oblivion secured in some protective arms. Sometimes the unconscious is glimpsed not in the depths but out in the open, as in the part of the session where the patient dramatizes and almost verbalizes his disquiet at being affected by the analyst from within. The patient goes so far as to tell us that if the session, like other experiences, leaves him with an uncomfortable feeling, he'll get rid of it like someone swatting a fly. He expresses the simple way he does this when he's in the car, by stepping on the accelerator and concentrating only on random traffic incidents. All of this, in the immediate reality of his discourse, is blurted out, in fast bursts, as the patient jumps from one thing to another. Then, he isn't aware of what he's doing, which is throwing himself into a verbal race without brakes, going so fast that the analyst won't be able to intervene and, if he manages to at some bend in the patient's discourse, the patient will accelerate a bit more, leaving the analyst again unable to speak. We therefore have another kind of transport here: the feared inside relation has been converted into a speeding external discourse that flees contact which is foreboded as an accident or crash.

The two-way direction of transfer that seems to characterize the analysand's experience should also be noted: The centrifugal direction going from unconscious and conscious fantasy to the present expression in the session; and the centripetal direction which is, in fact, the impact that the present situation in the session makes on the analysand's conscious and unconscious phantasy. The two processes are probably simultaneous and the present situation of the session which affects the patient and which he incorporates, is illuminated by the projection of unconscious representations in an ongoing sequence of introjections and projections. It will be useful to bear in mind this *bidirectionality of experience* when we relate transference and symbol.

I shall now go on to answer the first question more explicitly: what is transported or transferred from inside to outside, from internal objects to the analyst, from the unconscious to external reality, from the family situation to the analytical one, and so on? With this patient, from what we learn of him in these first sessions, we can see that what he transfers are feelings of unease, of persecution and ill-tolerated guilt. It is also clear that he makes use of a whole range of psychic processes consistent with old resorts of fleeing, shrugging things off and, still more, competing with his objects from other times with rational arguments, et cetera. In fact, what is transferred is a whole relational atmosphere and not only the drives, the basic impulses of love and hate. This is why Sigmund Freud, and later and more explicitly, Anna Freud, spoke of transference love and hate, and also of the transference of defences. In fact, all the contours of the old object relations, with their inherent impulses, emotions, and conflicts, are transported to the relationship with the analyst (see, here, an extensive discussion by B. Joseph, 1985).

Transference and symbolic function

In this paper, I'd like to reflect upon the nexuses of transference and symbolic function and, in particular, the following aspects:

a   affinities between the transferential link and the symbolic link;
b   the quality of the transference and of the symbolic formation that is established with it;
c   Eros and aggression, truth and lie in the fluctuations of the transference, and in the development and deterioration of the symbol.

In order to approach these three sections rigorously, it is necessary to deal with the concept of the symbol in the way I have dealt with transference. This turns out to be more difficult because, if transference is a notion derived from clinical facts and is exclusive to psychoanalytic elaboration, the concept of the symbol is, however, the heterogeneous result of a much broader spectrum of elaborations. These elaborations come not from the discipline of psychoanalysis alone, but rather from disciplines as diverse as philosophy, psychology, linguistics, anthropology, et cetera. It is true that, to these contributions, which are as old as culture itself, psychoanalysis has added some that are very original, namely the notion of *symbolization of the unconscious in a person's conscious fantasy, corporeality, or conduct*.

The fact that the symbol is the object of study of so many disciplines, needs to be borne in mind so that we are spared confusion over use of the term and can differentiate between supposed synonyms. One such differentiation is that which should be established between *symbol and sign*. In fact, the criteria don't always correspond from one discipline to the next, as we see on re-reading authors such as Saussure and Piaget, to cite the most classic examples. For some, the symbol, unlike the sign, would have a conventional relationship with the object it represents (as in codes or artificial languages) while, for others, this conventionalism would pertain to the sign, while the symbol would mean a nexus of morphic, functional, and structural correspondences between representor and represented.

For all the diversity of criteria, one common feature seems to prevail, whether we're speaking of signs or symbols, quintessences, analogies, or metaphors. All deal with meaning. Piaget seeks it in every mental element, starting from perceptions themselves. Meaning, understood as a relationship between signifier and signified, has particular connotations in psychoanalysis. Freud's *Bedeutung* is not that of the phenomenologists of his day and neither is it that of present logic.

However, in any sign or symbol we can find a quality of general validity if we consider, as F. Gantheret (1989) does, that the sign itself contains within it something that is absent. It conveys something that is not itself. The sign then supposes the relationship between a present, symbolizing object, and an absent object that is being indicated. As I noted above, this relationship may entail formal, functional, or structural analogies. A mere analogy of form is an iconic symbol, like breast and lemon, penis and mushroom. But the breast can also be represented by a fountain. Here, the iconic differences vanish, and it is the functional equivalent, the fount of life, that prevails. At other times, what is highlighted in this correspondence between representor and represented is, more than form and function, texture; the intimate structure of the two poles of the symbol. The more appropriate the symbol, the more the morphic, functional, and structural correlations concur.

In order to clarify matters, I have given some extremely simple examples in which a relationship between signifier and signified exists between two specific objects, for example, breast and lemon. But what we study in psychoanalysis are much more complex relationships between that which is present and absent, between symbolizer and symbolized. Each of them belongs to very different classes, as is the case of a mental object and a specific object. Hence, a person's cunning may be symbolized by a fox, or a mental state dominated by a mixture of love and hate can be signified by a hysterical muscle spasm. In this latter case, things have become much more complicated and the body, in an ambiguous position of immobility and tension, becomes a sign of a struggle between an aggressive impulse and the impossibility of giving expression to this impulse.

The characteristic of the symbol that most concerns us in psychoanalysis is that part, the symbolized, which is not within reach. It is unconscious, which means that the person who suffers the hysterical cramp or paralysis is faced with a signifier without a signified. It is the analyst who, with knowledge of the patient's story or private myth and his behaviour in the session, can connect the love–hate conflict, to stay with this schematic example, with its bodily expression, the muscular hypertonia. The conflict may also be translated into verbal or extra-verbal manifestations of doubt, and ambivalence towards the therapist and the treatment. In linking verbal and symptomatic motor conduct with the unconscious situation, the analyst establishes a relationship in which something from the present, the muscle spasm, is the symbolizer of something that is not apparent: the ambiguous attitude towards the therapist, the relationship of simultaneous love and hate towards an internal image, for example of the father or of the mother, that is suffused with emotion. By linking this unconscious representation, feelings, and the muscular manifestation in the here-and-now of the session, the analyst draws attention to a link that has hitherto not been apparent, but which in fact has been denied by the patient.

When we say, as Hanna Segal does, that by interpreting we proceed to the construction of the symbol, I want to express precisely that. In other words, we situate at an optimal distance two elements that were either too much separated, which is to say dissociated, or too close, which is to say confused. In some cases, interpretation brings together two elements which displacement or isolation or conversion had distanced, but on other occasions in a session, because of the reestablishment of a symbolic link, we proceed differently. Instead of bringing together two things that have been too far apart, we separate things that are too close, which is to say superimposed or confused. This is the case in those situations where, following an intervention, the patient experiences the analyst as so accusatory that he is filled with panic or pessimism regarding the future of the treatment. The rising emotion isn't alleviated until it has been possible to establish a distinction between the analyst's statement, which doesn't fit with the view or the desire of the analysand, and the image of a recriminatory, punitive internal object that is linked with childhood panic about being punished. In this case, the construction of the symbol proposed by the interpretation has had to proceed in a direction that is opposite to that which brought on the muscle cramp. Instead of bringing together two dissociated contents, two experiences that have been experienced as identical have had to be separated: the internal superego image and the attitude of the analyst which is compared with that of the unconscious primary object that has been reactivated by the analytical situation. Once the optimal distance is established, the link between the internal superego object and the present object, the analyst, becomes clearer. Aspects of the internal object are projected into the external analyst, but this does not mean that they are confused.

However, constructing the symbol through interpretation of the transference means not only establishing a link between two elements that are too far apart or too close, and situating them at an optimal distance from which they can relate. It also means that what was being linked clearly to ambivalence (muscle spasms, feelings of rejection, vomiting, anxiety over sexual abandon, terrifying fear of open spaces, of the analyst in the session and the blaming father, and so on), can be situated in an open nexus where there is room for different vectors of reciprocal signification. In all the cases just referred to, we might say, as Freud did, that one thing symbolizes another. But if we understand the symbol as a nexus, as being in an interactive relationship between symbolizer and symbolized, then strictly speaking we would have to talk about symbolic formations in which symbolizer and symbolized may coexist in a rigid relationship: analyst and father are felt to be the same thing, the breast is thought to be identical to the lemon, and open spaces of agoraphobia simply *are* an open field for imminent sexual abandon. In such cases, the symbolic function has the value of an equation, as Segal points out. Since in these examples, one thing is equal to another, an emotional atmosphere of anxiety about objects or situations comes into being.

Hanna Segal's great contribution was to show us, in a very didactic way, that the quality of the symbol is inextricably connected to the quality of object relations in the mind of the person who produces it. In a psychotic state, a lemon might awaken unease and emotion in a person because it is literally and specifically equated with a breast, and then the lemon can become a persecutory, fetishist, or phobic object. By contrast, for a person with more evolved object relations, squeezing a lemon will have no erotic or aggressive meaning, even though he or she might recognize the iconic analogy of fruit and breast.

To return to the situation of the analysis, we might say that in the interpretation, we attend to the transference relationship, or to the symbolization of an internal object by the analyst. Such interpretation may ease the patient's confusion, helping him to understand that the analyst is a representation and not an equation. The extremely emotive situations that appear in the analytical setting are, on the one hand, due to the transport, or massive transference of internal situations onto the relationship with the analyst. And, on the contrary, they may follow from the apparent lack of any transport from the intrapsychic relational situation to the here-and-now of the relationship with the analyst. The French, especially Maurice Bouvet, once used to speak of the situations I am discussing now as examples of resistance to transference, either because there is too much proximity or too much distance. Nowadays, we use other terms: acting-out, both in and outside the transference, transference psychosis, transference perversion, and so on. Indeed, in extreme cases we find that we are faced with the problem of finding the necessary optimal distance for a good construction of the symbol. The patient who doesn't consciously experience any feeling, who is unable to establish any analogical link between past and present experience and that which he might experience in the session, is in a senseless situation. He can find no resonance with his experience due the excessive splitting of his experiences. At the other extreme, the patient who so vividly takes the analyst for his father, has made such a massive projection of his internal object into the analyst that, for him, the analyst doesn't represent his father but *is* his father. Part of the patient is split off from the representation of himself and of his objects and is absolutely situated in the analyst, such that a very confused relationship is established with him. This is what Melanie Klein conceived as a narcissistic object relation. She also spoke of schizoid object relations. The patient in the earlier example deals with his internal conflict with the paternal object as if it was an external conflict with the analyst. The patient *is beside himself*, (and never has the expression been so apt), because he has transposed or transferred his internal object relation into the present reality of the therapeutic relationship.

When it has been possible to establish an optimal distance between the symbol and that which is symbolized, what opens up is an intermediary area where the two poles of the symbolic formation – in our case, the internal object and the analyst – are reciprocally signified in indefinite enrichment. When the analyst is not ineluctably the punitive father, he starts to become polysemic: as well as being punitive, at certain times he is credited perhaps with being afflicted, at other times as protective, seducible, et cetera. The emotional charge of the old relationship with the father can now be represented in the analytical relationship and, on the contrary, attitudes, reactions, or the temperament of the analyst bring out, in fantasy or in memory, other aspects of the image of the father. Hence, the transference setting begins to enrich this network of reciprocal significations between outside and inside, between internalized relations and the present of the relationship with the analyst. In a developing symbolic formation *bidirectionality between symbolizer and symbolized* becomes noticeable. Donald Meltzer has strongly emphasized this bidirectional character of symbol formation. In this regard, he is working along the lines of contributions made by Ernst Cassirer and, in some sense, by Freud. He is also of course returning to Hanna Segal in the sense that he acknowledges that the link between symbolizer and symbolized can adopt the different particularities of an object relation.

It is appropriate to indicate at this point the concordance between psychoanalytic conceptions of the symbol and the work of a good number of linguists who, when studying the structure of metaphor, accept the criterion of interaction, in contrast with that of comparison or substitution between the two subjects of the metaphor. This is the view, for example, of Max Black, a philosopher and linguist at Cornell University. To give an example, if we say, "Society is a jungle", the two subjects of the metaphor, *society* and *jungle*, are the two poles. Society is the literal pole and jungle the figurative one. What is expressed by linguists who ascribe to the theory of the interaction of words is that the metaphor, "Society is a jungle" would not have been established by a simple comparison or substitution of society by jungle. They think, as Max Black does, that "The metaphorical utterance works by *'projecting upon' the primary subject* a set of 'associated implications'... that are predicable of the secondary subject" (1993: 28, my emphasis).

With the metaphorical connection between society and jungle, some characteristics of wild nature, natural selection, struggle for life, survival of the fittest, cruelty, et cetera, are transported and projected until they impregnate the characteristics of human life in a community. Then again, we also realize that in experiencing or imagining the jungle, we do so by projecting into the representation that we have of it some aspects of our human experience.

The result is that, thanks to the metaphor, not only has society become ethological, Darwinian, and bestial but the jungle has become humanized or, better said, has been turned into society. Max Black reminds us of Ivor Armstrong Richards' impressive image, namely the *interanimation of words*, which expresses even more anthropomorphically a sort of exchange between the two images that mutually transcend and enrich each other, thus recalling the projective and introjective movements of the interpersonal relationship.

The aim of this paper is to specify the isomorphisms between symbolic formation (the metaphor, one might say) and the transference, where the latter is understood as an externalization, dramatization, and metaphorization of an intrapsychic relationship between the self and internal objects in the here-and-now of the analytic relationship. One might say that the analytic situation offers the best conditions for generating a symbol owing to the fact that it has the potential to create an optimal distance between the symbol and that which is symbolized. Thus, it works against confusion and dispersion. In fact, in both its external and formal aspects, and in the internal attitude of analyst and analysand, everything is ready for close proximity while simultaneously maintaining a distance. Proximity is encouraged by the analyst who invites the patient to free associate, and who facilitates the reaching to the surface of the unconscious. Distance is in turn assured by the renunciation of all acting in or acting out. For the analyst, this relinquishment finds its most demanding expression in Bion's postulation that the most ideal mental state for the analyst is that which is cultivated without memory or desire.

The conditions for treatment therefore facilitate this paradoxical confluence of physical and intersubjective proximity, but also of distance, which is guaranteed by rigorous restriction of reciprocal knowledge to the isolated coexistence of the session, which is limited to stringent visual and verbal contact. These ideal conditions, which are always threatened by actions within or outside the analytical relationship, coincide with those required by symbol formation, which is to say, putting things into a relation of enough proximity for them to link up, and enough distance for them not to be confused.

In these conditions of optimal distance, the free association of the analysand and his floating or evenly suspended attention, will foster the establishment of the accumulative nexuses I have spoken of. Then, the transference, in the broadest and most total sense, will keep expanding into a network of meanings between the internal object relations and the analyst–analysand relation. This means that symptomatic formations, repetitive compulsive actions, rituals of behaviour that we can understand as symbolic equations between unconscious phantasy and conduct, find within the framework of the treatment a way of vividly representing themselves in the different facets of the relationship with the analyst. To put it slightly differently, the symbolic equation of the symptom becomes a symbol in the strict sense to the extent that it is metaphorized into the more open possibilities of an interpersonal relationship.

I shall take as a paradigmatic example the case of a phobic patient. For him, the unconscious internal situation that brings on, for example, anxiety about narrow, dark streets and spaces isn't understood. He only knows that just thinking about these spaces makes him feel oppressed and suffocated. He has established a symbolic equation in which the two terms, narrow space and suffocation, are invariably brought together. The symbolic equation is a closed, saturated union that excludes any other meaning, which could expand the sense of either term of the equation. A street evokes another street, always with the same particularities of narrowness and darkness, and the same can be said of any other claustrophobic spaces like lifts, telephone boxes and so on.

However, if these same closed, saturated formations come to the setting and procedures of the analytic situation, the sessions themselves become a variation on the same theme. Then, there arise new and undefined possibilities for interaction, and for thinking about the meaning of it. Hence, for example and to continue with the phobic vignette, the dark narrow street or the lift starts to be linked with other narrow and closed spaces, like the body itself, including the body of the analyst. The narrowness and the darkness also come to be signifiers of mental qualities, like things the body doesn't make wholly transparent, such as the unknown of the feeling of the other. In the session, silence perhaps brings into relief the opacity of the analyst, and the unease that his anonymity awakens. The darkness is becoming a mental quality. The consulting room is well lit, but the oppression, bordering on asphyxiation, is felt in the session where the analyst has been experienced as hermetic and mysterious, as other hermetic and mysterious people in the patient's past. The powerful connection between narrow spaces on the one hand, and oppression and suffocation on the other, has slowly become a bundle of relations catalysed by present feelings, sensations, and phantasies that emerge in the course of the session. Now, dark narrow streets refer both to the impenetrable body of the mother, the uncertain intentionality of the analyst, and the analysand's fear about the course of his thinking and his unclear itinerary. If the analyst, in his silence full of unknowns, becomes representative of the dark intimacy of the parental couple, he is also, in phantasy, lying in wait in the dark narrow street. The patient is then urging him to move in a sort of repetitive compulsion. However, in felicitous moments, he is also the one who shows the patient that being lost in the dark does not mean being annihilated, but that one can come out of it, in Bion's style, with a meaningful and clarifying *"ray of darkness"*.

The initial, total equation of elements such as a lift or narrow street with oppression and suffocation, has now become a bundle of meanings that are never definitively bound. Instead, it has become possible to elaborate the nexuses that are circulating between the two poles of the equation, and which have become reciprocal representations (from bodily and the psychic, from outside and inside, from past and present, et cetera).

This process of transformation of a closed symbol, or symbolic equation, into an open symbol of meanings and perspectives, means that unconscious conflict has become metamorphized in the analytic situation. Dramatization of the conflict thus transports, transfers, and enables a reorganization that will free the patient from the determinism that once perpetuated his misfortune.

This remodelling is, as we know, a slow process. Opening up the most elemental symbolic formations is done slowly, zigzag style. Symbolization, and I shall emphasize this later, is clarifying but it can also offer deceptive meanings. What we can say, in any case, is that the ambiguity and the richness of the symbol in psychoanalysis has only been captured by way of analysis of the transference. Freud was only interested in the meaning of symptoms, the symbols of which had the symbolized as a pure substitute for their symbolizer, an obligatory substitute, a disguise for escaping censure and repression. This is why he thought they were unidirectional in the sense, for example, that the penis can be symbolized by a long object, but a long object cannot be symbolized by a penis. When Melanie Klein conducted one of her first analyses of a young child with the case of Fritz, she described a symptomatic translation of a symbolic equation and still continued to highlight the defensive value of the symbol. The child was terrified by an unconscious phallic object which became transposed upon many apparently undifferentiated objects like trees or telephone poles. The equation was so literal that the child couldn't go out because of the panic trees and poles inspired in him. They were the phallic objects they symbolized.

However, Freud discovered the transference in clinical work and, even before *The Interpretation of Dreams*, the analytic session was being outlined as a possible container of meanings that find expression and correspondence in the patient's conduct and discourse. Interpretation, Freud thought, could re-establish the nexuses of meaning that the defences had blocked. Some years later, in her theoretical and technical explanations, Klein expanded still more the symbolizing potentialities of the transference.

The relationship that is established between analyst and analysand in the particular conditions of their setting has a double value of symbolizing and symbolized. On the one hand, the patient's drama or internal conflict is represented in the setting of the session, and the present relation with the analyst symbolizes old relational situations that have pervaded his or her way of thinking, feeling, and perceiving the present reality. The session is the symbol of this internal state of affairs. Yet, at the same time, the present situation with the analyst, and often that which is least detected, is spontaneously symbolized in the form of behaviour, of phantasy, of memory, or of a new view of the patient's past. Then, we can say that the present reality of the session is not the symbolizer but the symbolized in the patient's productions.

What clinical psychoanalysis also shows us is that this construction of the symbol, in the sense of translation and evidencing of the unconscious, is laboriously done in a progressive convergence of our more or less disseminated emotional experiences. The assembly of our own ego implies fluctuations to avoid the suffering entailed by taking on our own truth. This then gives rise to a tangled dispute between *symbol* and *diabolon*, between integration and splitting, between differentiation and confusion. Coming into play is a whole dialectic between truth and lie and, in some sense, the struggle between the life drive and the death drive. Life and death, love and hate, truth and lie, are not presented as clearly outlined, contrasting classes of affect, dispositions or drives. Rather, they form a dense mesh. Just as Freud (1912) indicated that in the very nucleus of libido there was a certain destructive avidity, we can also conclude that truth and lie are interlinked. Going back to the symbol, one should caution that the plenitude of its formation and its indefinite capacity for meaning can deteriorate into forms of sectorization and dismemberment. It may become just one more univocal but fallacious, partial "truth". One might say that the symbol, in its rich ambiguity, also brings a certain unease, since it may be felt as chaotic, provoking anxious perplexity that is hard to bear. When this situation of perplexity becomes acute, the *false symbol* that is univocal, vehement, and saturated, may be offered to put an end to the suspense of uncertainty, while also serving a range of defence mechanisms.

In clinical practice, such deterioration of symbolic representative capacity which favours false symbols, is particularly apparent at fertile times in the treatment when formerly rigid patterns of behaviour and internal experience make way for broader perspectives. Then, experience is lived with more equanimity, but also takes on a disturbing ambiguity. New perspectives, though they awaken hope, are nuanced: they entail the recognition of error, of guilt perhaps, recognition of what has been lost, and they raise questions about where newly acquired truths might lead. This crossroads-type situation, in which one is faced with outdated truths *and* new perspectives that are both appealing and uncertain, is filled with ambivalence. It is an experience of "exacerbated vacillation" that has been described in several ways. León Grinberg for example, refers to it as being on a razor's edge, such is the dramatic fluctuation between depressive and persecutory feelings. If a longing for progress, in the sense of integration, wins the day, the patient is, though trepidatious, to some extent ready to face new situations. He can potentially face the return of what was once repressed. He enters the depressive position where mourning is elaborated. He grieves for his narcissistic omnipotence, begins to repair the objects of his love, and faces all the insecurity entailed by this new situation. If, on the contrary, anxiety is too strong and indomitable, which is to say when fear becomes unspeakable, "nameless" dread, to use Bion's term, then, from the razor's edge the patient opts to regress, to remain anchored for a time, weighing up the pros and cons, haggling before making a commitment to the new truth. Sometimes such regressions are brusquely expressed in the form of a negative therapeutic reaction.

This very narrow mental space described by Grinberg, which may see an abrupt shift from a depressive to a persecutory state, also entails the replacement of creative, symbols that illuminate inner reality, by partial truths or false symbols. If the construction of a true symbol is laborious, its degradation, as with anything that is destructive, can be very quick, and involves the resort to denial and fragmentation of perceived and psychic reality.

However as we know, in the course of a satisfactory therapeutic process, such ups and downs of integration and disconnection are usual. As soon as one approaches truth one may withdraw, confronted as one is with the great anxiety that truth awakens. Even so, despite all the *diabolons*, we keep coming closer to a cumulative establishment of symbolic formation. When, regardless of depressive and persecutory anxieties, dreams and experience, desire and reality, do become reciprocal signifiers; when the past evoked in the session illustrates the immediacy of the lived present; when the incipience of this present facilitates the emergence of a past that has been ignored or rejected, and when logical flow and magical thinking find a happy concurrence, then and only then can we talk about having initiated the construction of the polyvalent symbol. Only then have we enlarged meaning in a poetic and rich sense, as is conveyed by the German word *Dichtung*. It is then that the experience of the psychoanalytic session acquires the feel of a certain, but fleeting plenitude, of the recovery of something that was once lost, and also of *Darstellung*, of figuration and presence of the absent, as if the word could suddenly contain everything that throbbed in the ongoing sequence of still formless experience.

Note

1 Published in *Revista Catalana de Psicoanàlisi*, vol. IX, n. 1–2.

Bibliography

Bion, W. R. (1962) A theory of thinking, *International Journal of Psychoanalysis*, vol. 43.

Bion, W. R. (1970) *Attention and Interpretation*, Tavistock Publications, London.

Black, M. (1993) More about metaphor, in Andrew Ortony (ed.) *Metaphor and Thought*, Cambridge University Press (1st edition 1979).

Bouvet, M. (1995) *Oeuvres psychoanalitiques (1948–1960)*, vol. II, *Résistances transfert*, Payot (1968).

Coromines, J. (1980–1991) *Diccionari etimològic i complementari de la Llengua Catalana*, Caixa de Pensions la Caixa.

Freud, A. (1936) *El yo y los mecanismos de defensa*, Paidos, Buenos Aires (1949).

Freud, S. (1900) *La interpretació dels somnis*, ch. 8, Empúries (1985).

Freud, S. (1912) *Zur Dynamik der Übertragung. Gesammelte Werke*, VIII, Imago, London (1943).

Freud, S. (1920) *Més enllà del principi del plaer*, Espais S.A., Barcelona (1989).

Gantheret, F. (1989) L'Originaire: La metaphore inaccomplie. Lecture given at the Institute of Psychoanalysis, Barcelona, February 1989.

Grinberg, L. (1978) The razor edge, *International Journal of Psychoanalysis*, vol. 59, Parts 2–3.

Joseph, B. (1985) Transference: The total situation, *International Journal of Psychoanalysis*, 66.

Klein, M. (1921) The development of a child, in *The Writings of Melanie Klein*, vol. I, Hogarth Press, London (1975).

Klein, M. (1946) Notes on some schizoid mechanisms, in *The Writings of Melanie Klein*, Vol. 111, Hogarth Press, London (1975).

Medina, J. (1989) El símbol i el diable. La vida i la mort. Una lectura filológica de l'Evangeli segons sant Joan, *Serra d'Or*, April.

Meltzer, D. (1983) *Dream Life*, ch. 5, Clunie Press.

Piaget, J. (1945) *La formation du symbole chez l'enfant*, Delachaux et Niestié.

Segal, H. (1975–1979) Notes on symbol formation, in *The Works of Hanna Segal*, ch. 2, pp. 49–65, Jason Aronson (1981).

Segal, H. (1991) *Dream, Phantasy and Art*, Routledge, London.

5 Notes about Imitation, Hypocrisy, and Transference Love[1]

Pere Folch Mateu

1 Introduction

The complex interaction of love and hatred, the clinical corollary of the elemental conflict between the life and the death drives, unfolds in a variety of ways during the course of a wide range of human relationships, and in particular in the vicissitudes of amorous relationships. The fluctuations and contrasts that are characteristic of such relationships, and their surprising dynamics, led Freud (1914, 1921) to the conclusion that falling in love had pathological, or at least abnormal components.

One collateral variant of this love–hate interaction is the complex coexistence of truth and deception. Freud (1905, 1910) repeatedly grapples with the coexistence of these opposites, both at a metapsychological and at a clinical level. On the one hand he took into account the sadistic elements inherent in libido, elements that express themselves in the manifest conduct of someone in a state of passionate arousal. He also noted the many types of aggressive reactions to frustration, in particular frustration inflicted on the individual by the object of their love. In later works (1921), Freud also grapples with a less tempestuous but more intense and tenacious attitude, experienced by the loving subject as submission, enslavement or amorous servitude (*verliebte Wirigkeit*). The obvious ambiguity and the mysterious incoherence of such love-related situations prompt Freud to raise questions about the authenticity of the love being professed.

Reflecting on this thorny question of authenticity, we find ourselves dealing with the interwovenness of truth and deception. The authenticity or truthfulness of the feelings and attitudes of the lovers, the *Echtheit* or *Wirigkeit* that Freud describes, depend, to my mind, on the particular way in which love and hate coexist in the conscious and unconscious mind of the subject.

I wish to make clear that neither the coexistence, nor the complex nature of these impulses implies inauthenticity. On the contrary, being able to tolerate and accept the inevitable mixture of love and aggression that is an inherent part of all relationships is a sign of the intensity and depth of the amorous experience. It is what will later permit the continued elaboration

DOI: 10.4324/9781003342472-5

of the associated conflicts: objectal versus narcissistic interests, exaltation of the object's value versus envy, yearning for proximity versus the anxiety of separation, etc.

It is actually in situations where there is neither a harmonious nor a tormented coexistence of love and hate, that we find amorous conduct to be inauthentic. In these apparently quite placid situations, there is nothing that evokes a sense of the constant inter-animation of bipolar impulses, with their frequent reciprocal excesses and compensations. On the contrary, it is a declaration of absolute availability to the other, from which the subject strives to eliminate every other feeling that might stand opposed to it. This "pure" love, free of foreign ingredients, fluctuates in intensity and duration, but while it lasts, the protagonist seems not to tolerate the slightest flaw in their idealized image of the object of their love, nor the slightest evidence of lukewarmness or confusion in their feelings. This idealization entails an attitude which seeks to avoid, at all costs, conflict with other sentiments that do not conform entirely with their predominant amorous fervour. To this end, the individual perpetuates the cleavage or splitting that keeps love and aggression at bay. A distance from unwanted feelings is maintained by their continuous denial, by means of refusal, repudiation, rejection, and foreclosure, with varying results. Sometimes the expulsion of aggressive impulses seems to be so decisive that the relationship with the object of love does not suffer. Even when the aggression might overflow into other relationships, it seems to pose no threat to the connection with the idealized object. But it is often the case that love and hate cannot be separated so completely. Then, what has been repressed, avoided or extirpated finds a way of invading the conscious mind and seriously threatening the apparently unconditional love. It is precisely then that the individual may resort to unconscious and conscious mechanisms to re-establish the splitting which translates into a more or less obvious falsifying attitude.

In the present notes I shall limit myself to considering the strategies deployed by patients in the course of largely favourable analytical processes. During different stages of their therapy, these patients behave in ways which we would interpret as psychic mimesis, imitation, and hypocrisy. Even when these behaviours are associated with unconscious motivations and goals, imitation and hypocrisy are the result of a more conscious intention.

I shall try to show the evolution that I have often been able to verify in such cases; the point of departure being an enthusiastic imitation of an idealized analysis and analyst. This enthusiasm can be seen to wane, painfully, as more and more insight is obtained. Early idealization recedes and is replaced by a conscious determination to adapt to the principles of a more realistic analysis, and to take on board the painstakingly acquired new truth.

It seems to me that the clinical facts that I am considering here have more than tangential links with the story of a little hero of a novel by Max

Beerbohm, inspired by an ancient oriental myth. The story of the *Happy Hypocrite*, for all its naivety, seems to me to represent a paradigm of certain processes of identification that are maintained alongside a conscious and tenacious determination to reproduce in a first-person narrative the attributes and ideals of the amorous object.

2 Imitation and Mimetism in the Analytical Situation

In these notes my starting point is a particular type of attitude displayed by certain patients during the course of analytical treatment. They are patients with a range of symptoms and attributes, which are particularly frequent among patients who intend to become psychotherapists or psychoanalysts themselves.

Such patients typically throw themselves into the treatment with admiration and fervour, convinced of the efficacy of psychoanalysis. Sometimes we are surprised by their easy adaptation to the technical guidelines and frame of the therapy. They seem to revel in the method and practice of free association. They extend the "psychoanalytical" atmosphere beyond the sessions with forays into self-analysis and derive pleasure from the amusing discovery of new meanings in every kind of situation, a phenomenon that Julia Kristeva described as "the festival of significance".

These patients could be likened to those who experience a psychoanalytical "honeymoon", who exhibit a "love of transference", but they differ from such honeymooners in that their fervour and enthusiasm does not centre exclusively on the figure of the therapist but overflows into the frame, the features of the method, the literature and the very institution of psychoanalysis. Even if, sooner or later, it is realized that this is not the whole picture, what they say and do seems to correspond to a deep-seated enthusiasm, whether or not this is dependent on the need to elude anxiety by means of total identification with an admired object (the psychoanalyst, psychoanalysis itself, or the setting).

Other patients do not exhibit such a fervent or constant attitude. They follow with interest the initial vicissitudes of the analysis and attempt not only to fine-tune their receptive attention, but also to imitate and replicate formal aspects of the analyst's interventions, in particular his or her vocabulary. They try to translate into "psychoanalytical" language their everyday experiences, thus taking refuge in their learning; or they use the same turns of phrase as the therapist, whether the latter has used some technical term or the more informal expressions of everyday speech. Whether they imitate the technical language of the analyst or a popular expression, what we observe is an attitude which expresses admiration and fear in equal measure. This actually betrays a lack of perceptive resonance on the patient's part, which prevents them from translating into their own words what they receive as external introjection, and which seems to induce submissiveness.

Apart from this imitative attitude, with its widely acknowledged intentionality, there is another attitude that we can observe in a third group of patients, also evident at times at the beginning of the analytical process. It is characterized by an adaptation to the analytic contract that seems to us to be imitative and artificial. The patient tries to conceal their scepticism, though the treatment does not live up to their expectations. They are patients who, despite their barely contained disillusionment, continue diligently and without fail to endure the vicissitudes and rhythm of the sessions, animated by the unshakable hope that their treatment will one day become as wonderful as the ideal image they have forged, in private, of psychoanalysis, that prompted them to decide to seek treatment.

A certain number of these patients, and professional psychologists, are motivated by their experience of conflict and their symptoms, and by their professional training. It is not uncommon for such patients to resort to psychoanalytical treatment after being disappointed by the results of other therapies: drugs, bioenergetic therapy, conduct modification treatments, etc. Converts to psychologism, they come to analysis as if under the impulse of a new faith.

We are discovering more and more about the conduct and structure of inauthentic personalities, and mimetic behaviours or "as if" personalities. They are patients who come across as having rigidly adopted patterns of opinion and conduct that cannot tolerate inflexions, who reduce every new experience to their habitual ideological schemata. They contrast with personality types that are characterized by a more versatile mimetism. In fact, the same subject might display different personality traits depending on the environment they happen to be in. A literary example of this changing personality, which flips from one attitude to another, is the protagonist of Aldous Huxley's novel *Two or Three Graces*.

These "as if" personalities, dominated as they are by extreme or cold mimetism, have been studied and reported to some degree following an original study by H. Deutsch. However, the subject of imitation and hypocrisy has not been thoroughly addressed in the psychoanalytical literature, and even less clarity surrounds the psychoanalytical status of such behaviours, that is to say, regarding their structural substrate. Based on my experience, I deduce that mimetism, imitation, and hypocrisy are articulated variously during the course of therapy, and it is especially at the beginning of treatment that they are presented in a more obvious manner with all their distinctive and characteristic features.

It is probably not only the imprecise correspondence of the descriptive level with the meta-psychological that obstructs the psychoanalytical connection between imitation and hypocrisy. Despite these behaviours having been linked to the underlying process of identification, and particularly to frustrated or distorted aspects of identification, the varied nature of the subject's intentions and aims has not been sufficiently acknowledged. Imitation, for example, has been too quickly assimilated to the authentic, and hypocritical behaviour has often been seen as deliberately intended, and as aiming to deceive. Despite the prevailing conviction that love and hate are inextricably bound up together in the dynamics of an inter-personal relationship, both imitation and hypocrisy have too readily acquired pejorative connotations.

This assessment highlights prejudices which influence the attitude of the analyst. In fact, the way in which imitative and hypocritical attitudes are explicated and interpreted can derive from moralistic countertransferential reactions. It is true that, from W. Stekel onwards, the analyst has had to be careful not to deem as "bad faith" deliberately insincere behaviour, reser-vation or ambiguity, or indeed the conscious concealment of the truth or mythomaniac activity on the part of the patient. The level of conscious-ness, and with it, the degree of responsibility attributed to the patient have influenced our understanding of the disorder and the interpretative sche-mata applied to it; the analyst can come across as being inclined to focus on the patient's level of consciousness, even when the latter is in the throes of distressing symptoms; or as seeing a perverse determination to cling to error, without taking into account the deep-seated motivations which cause the patient to behave in a certain way. On the other hand, the analyst is fully convinced of the difficulty every patient, and indeed every human being, has in withstanding certain doses of reality and truth.

A broad spectrum of falsifications of reality is deployed in the course of every analytical process. With no intention to classify such falsifications of the truth, I shall only point out that they may be effected both afferently, or in other words through particular features of the patient's receptive style (or via his perception of external and internal reality), and efferently, that is through their expressive system as a whole. Bion speaks of the self-deception which follows from a particular way of perceiving, which may lead to a fragmented and mystified representational organization. To this falsification of external reality, one might add a certain mystification in the perception of internal reality, and indeed the fraudulent expression of this reality in every kind of lying to and deceiving other people, for whatever reason.

An exacting classification would have to distinguish not only the ways in which falsifying behaviour is perceived and expressed, but also the level of consciousness within which perception and expression occur. From a more or less dream-like state, to an indisputable mythomaniac attitude; from openly declared transvestite play to the deliberate desire to hide the truth or mislead, the level of consciousness is aleatory. As stated previously, we should also take into account the aims and motivations which lead someone to misrepresent internal or external reality, the anxi-eties which might induce someone to fantasize, and the impulses which give rise to a falsifying attitude.

A hypocritical attitude is often assumed to result exclusively from an aim to defraud, out of conscious and deliberate intentionality. But the analyst should bear in mind, among other things, two types of hypocritical behaviour: (a) that which is guided by the intention to conceal greed, envy, and the desire to control the object of one's admiration, and (b) that which is motivated by the desperate need to be accepted and loved, under the painful conviction that no one could possibly tolerate, and much less love, what one feels to be one's own flaws, badness or insecurity. In the former case, what predominates is the drive to destroy; in the second, it is the need to love and to be loved.

The legend of *The Happy Hypocrite* helps us to reflect once again on the broad spectrum of attitudes governed by falsehood, from imposture to self-deception. The essential meaning of all the variants of falsehood can only be grasped by bearing in mind the level of consciousness of the subject, his motivations and the aims out of which it arises. As this legend seems to me to allude to the attitudes that develop in the course of certain analyses, I shall summarize it briefly before returning to clinical problems.

3 The Myth of the Sanctified Hypocrite

I know about this myth through the version of it provided by Max Beerbohm, comic writer, critic and caricaturist, in his novel *The Happy Hypocrite*, published in 1897 and disseminated with great success several years later.

The hero of the story is Lord George Hell, a depraved and cruel aristocrat in his thirties. He had led a scandalous life of gambling and orgies, and had an almost satanic reputation dating from his adolescence. Specifically, at the age of 17 he had won the ancestral home of a friend whom he had then reduced to destitution. In fact, he had won this bet by cheating with loaded dice.

He would frequent the nocturnal haunts of brigands and libertines in the company of a notorious, perverted dancer. He was particularly fond of a venue which had a little theatre where the most scandalous spectacles imaginable were staged. It was there that he was captivated by a shy, pale, young debutante dancer, who struck him as being incongruously timorous and virginal in this setting.

Lord George was deeply moved. Cut to the quick and passionately in love, he had the young girl introduced to him. He fell to his knees before her and humbly implored her to marry him. The girl, somewhat confused but decisive, said after listening to his pleas: "Monsieur, I thank you for your beautiful words, but I can never be your wife. I shall never be the wife of a man who does not have the face of a saint. Your face, Monsieur, reflects, I have no reason to doubt, true love for me, but it is a mirror that is also tarnished by the vanities of this world ... To the man whose face is as luminous as the face of the saints I shall give my true love ..."

Deeply distressed by this delicate refusal, but spellbound by the girl's radiant beauty, Lord George felt that he, and everything else in the world, had suddenly changed. He rediscovered the enchantment of nature and realized that an unbridgeable distance now separated him from the life of luxury that he had been living.

A few days later, he passed in front of the shop owned by Mr. Aeneas, a famous mask-maker whose reputation was shrouded in mystery and myth, as he had provided a mask for the Sun himself, the great god Apollo. The mask he had made for him was of matt silver, and with it the Sun was able to spy on the actions of humankind when he came out for a stroll at night. He could only do this at night, because when he appeared during the day men would leave their beds and their orgies and go to work. And so, the sun was disheartened to realize that he could not observe what he had been told about humankind's nocturnal delights. Now, with his mask on, men did not realize that it was often Apollo who watched them during the night, and instead imagined that it was a pale goddess. However, the sun needed to keep getting the mask remade because eventually each would melt. Vulcan made the first one, then Mercury, but after that he had to resort to mask-makers. Aeneas receives no pay from the Sun, because the gods of Olympus don't pay, but in exchange for his work Apollo rewards Aeneas by granting that the wax masks he makes never melt in intense heat.

In response to a request from our hero, the mask-maker showed him a beautiful saint's mask which he kept hidden in a special place. "Is this saint's mask the perfect reflection of true love?", Lord George asks. He tries it on, and after asking Aeneas to make some adjustments because he found the mask rather too contemplative, the latter complied and fitted the mask so seamlessly that it became a perfect disguise. He looked at himself in a mirror, and felt transformed, as if his past had been nothing but a dream. His voice sounded strange through his lips which were concealed behind the wax mask. However, his former mistress, who was loitering on the street outside the shop, asked him to give her the little bouquet of flowers that he was holding. Lord George told her that he did not know her. Despite a certain feeling of anxiety, he headed decisively for the young girl, Jenny Mere, to introduce himself to her, convinced that she would love him with his new face. And so she did. The girl was captivated, and to cut a long story short, a prolonged amorous idyll began. They moved into a cabin in the middle of the forest, and Lord George gave away his immense fortune, made restitution to the friends he had betrayed and retained only a small part of his wealth. Then, he devoted himself wholeheartedly to his new bucolic life with his beloved. At times, when he lay down beside a river and saw the image of his mask reflected in it, he felt ashamed of having deceived the young girl, but he said to himself that though the mask was a contemptible ploy, perhaps it was also a symbol of sincere repentance and love. But the young girl was falling deeper and deeper in love with the face of the saint and Lord George ended up forgetting that he was deceiving her.

Time passed happily by. It was only when he was asleep that Lord George would have strange nightmares. Though he was afraid that the wax mask might prove to be a barrier between himself and his wife, with the passing of time he no longer felt it covering his face, and it seemed to him that the mask had become an integral part of him.

One day the couple realized they had been married for many months, and felt that they should celebrate this. However, while they were organizing the meal in the garden, Lord George's former perverted lover reappeared in a state of wild fury, determined to unmask him and wreck his happiness. After a very tense scene she said to him, "Plaster saint, I have come to unmask you!" Lord George wanted to get rid of her, in front of the astonished gaze of the young Jenny, but his former mistress, far from leaving, lunged at him and ripped off his mask. But, to her astonishment, the face behind the mask was exactly the same as the mask, line by line, feature by feature: it was the face of a saint! The woman left, bewildered, and Lord George, unaware of the miracle that had just occurred, told his wife that he would leave. He was repentant and ashamed, and told her she should forget him. The girl, who did not understand any of this, said: "Why did you try to win my heart with a mask? Why did you imagine that I would love you less tenderly if I saw your own face? He looked into her eyes ... and he saw reflected in them the tiny image of his face ... Your beauty is precious to me, and I like it better than the image which covered it and deceived me ... You did right by covering from me the splendour of your face, as I was not worthy to see it before now ... But now I am your wife. Let me contemplate your true features for ever more ... Kiss me with your true lips". Now they were alone in the garden. And the mask was no longer lying on the ground. The sun had melted it.

4 Imitation, Hypocrisy and the Relationship with the Object

Imitation occurs at very different levels of consciousness, from the most elemental levels of primary imitation, inherent in the apperceptive function, to meticulously premeditated imitative behaviours. Imitation therefore reflects an intimate attitude which is perfectly in keeping with a desire to be like the object. On the other hand, hypocrisy is an intentional behaviour which aims to conceal an internal attitude. This often translates into an ambiguous or affected appearance, but hypocritical individuals can also exhibit an appearance of enthusiasm for values and persons, even as they conceal a contrary interior attitude. The hypocrite uses imitation to make others believe they have what they do not have, and are what they are not.

A., a borderline patient, began his therapy with enthusiastic admiration for psychoanalysis, on account of its possibilities and its practice. In order to neutralize his intense persecutory anxiety, he quickly made a superficial identification with me, which served to pacify him for a while. However, his anxiety soon acquired a delusional tone, to the point where he had to be admitted, entirely with his consent, to a psychiatric hospital. There, I was informed, he heard opinions that were strongly opposed to psychoanalysis, and which worried him greatly. A. told me that he was very surprised that I had "thrown him to the lions". I visited him every day, and as he knew at what time I would be coming, he came to meet me at the door, anxious to warn me about the danger I was in there, as an openly declared psychoanalyst. Although the institution in question was notorious for its organically-oriented spirit, and the assistants working there were somewhat sceptical about psychoanalysis, there was no doubt as to the delusional nature of the patient's interpretation. He told me that he had been extremely discreet, had pretended not to have any interest in psychoanalysis, and had in this way managed to keep out of trouble.

In fact, the crisis which gave us no option but to have the patient hospitalized began when he became unable to keep at bay his own negative feelings about psychoanalysis, which were undermining his idealization of it. Once admitted to the clinic, he used the anti-psychoanalytic character of the institution to project into it his anxiety attacks, and the distrust he felt towards me. This situation was very much alive in the patient's own psychic reality, when he felt that his action towards me triggered within him a destructive envy. When this situation could be understood and articulated, he calmed down as he could see that I could survive; his persecution complex waned, and he was able to leave the clinic and continue his treatment with me. The memory of this case occurred to me because it exemplifies the coexistence of imitation and hypocrisy, when the latter is aimed at denying an enthusiastic fusion with the ideal object.

In this episode involving the "persecutory" institution, Patient A. exemplified what in more stable patients occurs when the psychoanalytical "honeymoon" is disrupted, after the first interpretations of manic fusion with psychoanalysis trigger and actualize negative aspects of transference. The relationship with the analyst then enters a more realistic phase, more conducive to an exploration of conflict. But the patient can try to elude this by deploying a hypocritical attitude, and clinging to a beatific relationship with another internally idealized object, now that the analyst has ceased to embody this object.

In the case of imitative attitudes which appear at the beginning of psychoanalytical treatment, what predominates is the very conscious desire to be like the admired object. There is no doubt that in this admiration, highly idealized aspects of one or several internal objects are projected into the analyst and the psychoanalytic method. But at the same time there is an over-enthusiastic response which issues from the unique, unprecedented experience of the conditions under which the treatment is framed, and from the benevolent and sympathetic attitude of the analyst. This experience engenders a desire to be functionally like the analyst. This mental state corresponds to what Widlöcher describes, with certain misgivings, as a desire for identification, the joy of being like the other, which nevertheless does not entail the desire to replace him or her, but rather a vibrant participation in the whole of the admired object (see Widlöcher 1968, pp. 147–149).

At this point we find ourselves quite close to the idea of a form of narcissism which, far from being animated by an intolerance of the greatness or goodness of the object, and far from denigrating it with projective attacks of jealousy, actually exalts the greatness of the object. The patient then aspires to becoming fused with the object, the analyst, in a longing to surpass their own limitations. It is reflective of a narcissism that is more libidinal than destructive. M. Klein occasionally referred to it in her work when discussing the relationship with the introjected ideal object, and it is also what Rosenfeld represents in his concept of libidinal narcissism. It is the same kind of narcissism that gives rise to certain aspects of creativity and which, far from being an autistic interiorization, engenders oceanic openness to the outside. It is the narcissism that F. Gantheret (1990) describes in his inspired study on Rilke, and which leads the individual "not to withdraw from the world, not to curl up within themselves, but in going out into the world, to fuse their identity with the world's objects. Wounded, insecure narcissism has thus turned towards life, instead of withdrawing from life".

It is this yearning to be part of the object, to savour it, and to become the object itself, without entirely nullifying oneself, that can feed into the kind of pantheistic or nirvana-oriented outlooks that are associated with predominantly libidinal narcissism. This tendency is exacerbated in anguish-inducing situations, but it also spurs the epistemophilic drive and the creative process. This might be described as, for example, the gestation accomplished in poetic discourse explored by Gantharet (1990, pp. 131–132). The narcissistic ideal of an always perfectible oneness has nothing to do with psychopathology, and complicates the ambiguous terminology of narcissism. Because, in fact, far from being a retreat within oneself, a shrinking of the self, it is an immersion in the object, empathic rather than controlling. Perhaps there is a desire for a temporary fusion with the other, or with the thing, but the aim is to emerge from this fusion and, so to speak, to glorify the object with all the vividness of the poetic word. The poet takes the risk of "peeling off their fragile skin and indwelling the thing: and then returning with the word. In poetic time ... there is this mystery: that the word can be *the thing made present* which emerges, and we within it, merged with it, *knowing it* with an unfamiliar knowledge, which is not knowing *about* it, but a fresh knowledge of the thing, and of ourselves in fusion with it".

The other vignette I have chosen to illustrate the dynamics of imitation and hypocrisy comes from the case of a patient whose pathology is not as severe as that of patient A. Perhaps at certain unconscious levels he suffers from a regressive need for fusional identification, but his outward behaviour corresponds to a subject–object distinction.

B. is a patient aged under 30 who started analysis because of a relationship issue, which had become critical. B had sufficient intuition to sense that it was a repetition of previous situations to which he had felt compulsively and uncontrollably drawn. He had quite a superficial intellectual knowledge of psychoanalysis, but it was enough to awaken his curiosity and give him hope. In the first sessions he said that from the very first interview, just before the holidays, he had already begun to feel better. He looked forward eagerly to the first sessions, in which I limited myself to listening to him and hinting at partial meanings from the range of content that he expressed. I noticed very soon that he was beginning to focus on tiny details that caught his eye in my consulting room, or on aspects of his own reactions. One day, for example, while I was buzzing the door open for him, he got distracted and had to ring the bell a second time. He said he had been distracted because he had noticed that the door had two locks, one on the right and the other on the left. In the waiting room he said, "I thought that my not having been attentive, and getting distracted, that you had to open the door for me twice, must have some meaning". He describes himself as being very busy with many things to deal with and as having difficulty avoiding becoming distracted. However, he tries to devote two or three quarters of an hour a day to his son. He remarks, "perhaps it's not much time, but it's intense engagement with him ..." He also comments on how much he likes being able to talk about everything in the sessions, about so many different experiences in his life, and to feel that he can be himself in so many situations, as if he is one single territory with many different spaces ... Then he describes a dream he had during the holiday: he was looking at a picture of the wedding of his parents and he saw that he was in the photo instead of his father. After a short pause he said that the dream had left a deep impression on him and stirred memories of many unpleasant experiences with his father. He said, "but I'm aware that it's a very clear dream, and I'm wondering if I might be trying to ... *please* ... *flatter* the analyst. "Please" and "flatter" were not common words in his vocabulary, but I had used them several days before to signal his fear that I might lose interest in him. I had been referring to his desire to revitalize the sessions with topics that I might be interested in, which prompted him to raise a current intellectual issue. When I told him in the last session that the fear of displeasing me was probably still strong, and that this fear showed itself when he referred to situations that confirmed previous interpretations, I added that he did this in a docile manner, not only repeating comments of mine, but also using words which were not common in his own vocabulary. The patient was angry and hurt and said, "so I imitate you, do I? As if that wasn't the most natural thing in the world! I'm just beginning this process, so I have to support and help myself with what I know is right ..." It seemed to me that he did not value, in my first intervention and the one that followed, my interest in showing him that he was not allowing himself to think otherwise or in another style, in accordance with the particular resonance that previous interpretations might have awakened in him. The patient had by no means interpreted me as being ironic in my observation, which I was afraid he might. In fact, I did think for a moment that he might have felt hurt in his childish vanity. On the contrary, however, he did not complain about being treated like a child who imitates, but actually claimed the right of a child who can only establish their identity through imitation.

Some months later, the same patient's initial enthusiasm started to wane. He remained very interested in analysis, but he became disconcerted and wearied as he became more and more aware of his ambivalence. He felt that things had changed. "At first it seemed to me that I was steaming ahead, and that you had to follow me, and in fact you were following me, but now I feel that I'm struggling to keep up with you".

The episode that I am about to report took place the day after a particularly gruelling session, in the wake of his difficulties in establishing himself in his university department. It was prompted by his desire to improve his status, but also by his scruples about competing with colleagues. The patient was able to engage with thoughts about old rivalries in his family, and with me in the transference. Comparisons between the three situations – his childhood, his professional setting and the present analytical situation seemed to overwhelm him. He told me that, like in an avant-garde theatre, I was making him jump from one of these three simultaneous scenarios to another, and that it was "an uphill struggle". The next day he arrived punctually, but he seemed stressed, almost breathless, with a rapid and interrupted flow of speech flow. He was wanting to engage in dialogue, even though there were moments when he seemed to be speaking to himself.

Patient B said, "After all the things I have had to deal with this morning, I had a headache when I got home. Perhaps it's not that I have taken on too much, but it's hard to go from one place to another: you finish a lecture and then you have to be available for the audience, you make a study plan and you have a whole series of bureaucratic issues to attend to … or you have to follow a course of study with students; yesterday evening I didn't stop until I was finally able to land in front of the television, where it's one disaster after another: the terrible tragedy in Kurdistan, with so many people dying due to being exposed to the elements".

Then he described a dream he had had the night before. It is a simple dream, virtually a single image: "I was going to your home, and just before I started to head up Musitu street, I realized that something had changed dramatically: what is still no more than a building site had become an almost completed house, there were no more barriers, and I could take up residence on the first floor, which was fully furnished and ready for me to move in. I was very surprised, because the reality is so different. It's not even possible to know whether they are still clearing the rubble or have begun to lay the foundations".

The story continued at a rapid pace with B describing his daily ordeals in a somewhat mournful tone. He felt uncomfortable addressing the discrepancy between dream and reality. I felt the need to intervene, as I was finally uncomfortable only to be listening. I had the feeling that he was alluding to the painstaking task of analysis when he mentioned the many issues he had to deal with. The patient's acceleration prompted me to help him by conveying a certain urgency to share his difficulty. It was in this context that I came up with the first interpretation.

ANALYST: In the midst of all this stress and tiredness, [the dream] offers something that is already fulfilled and completed. I think that, as on other occasions, you are comparing these "uphill" sessions with the street and this new building; you are also separating yourself from the rubble of old patterns and problems, but the treatment is not providing you with the rapid transformation you had hoped for. By contrast, in the dream everything is ready for you to enjoy this transformation.

PATIENT B: (Brief silence) ... I think that yes, things are going slowly, and it's hard ... I suffer because everything seems ready, but yet there is still so much to do ... well, you say that this task is an uphill struggle, like climbing Musitu street, but, in fact, the building under construction gives onto another street behind it, Bertran street, so it does not only belong to one street ... (Pause).

ANALYST: Indeed, the house being built has two sides, and undoubtedly the dream has more than one facet ... maybe you felt that I was going too quickly when I interpreted one aspect of the dream.

PATIENT B: I don't know ... this house in the dream, or rather the first floor, reminds me of the first floor of my Department; there I would like to be installed to finally take a rest from competitions and official exams .... Then I would have no problem ... well, I would have problems, but I would feel supported.

ANALYST: Now I'm thinking that with this other side of the building, you can tell me that a finished house is better, and that this laborious task of demolishing and rebuilding something, you feel is old and painful ... the shortest route would be to take refuge in existing patterns ... so it would not be a matter of building your own way of thinking and feeling, but of seeking support and adapting to a model provided by the Institution ...That is happening after yesterday's session, when you felt overwhelmed because you thought I was pressing you to consider so many different scenarios in your life ... that caused you to lose your footing, and, in the dream, to opt for a mould of already established patterns ...

For patients who have undergone analysis with didactic aims in mind, the Institute of Psychoanalysis is often seen as a completed and well-ordered installation which offers univocal patterns in terms of its effective regulations. This is in contrast with the vague and ambiguous mobility characterizing the first stages of the analytical process. The hope and excitement of the first few months however, soon begins to weaken. When treatment is going well, the idealization of the analyst and the frame cannot remain so compact, but the unverified remoteness of the Institute means that the high expectations with which they come to the consulting room can be displaced onto it.

I have selected vignettes corresponding to the two cases (patients A and B), with a view to getting closer to the phenomenon of imitation in patients with different symptomatic profiles, and very different psycho-pathological substrates. However, in both cases, intentionality and imita-tive action were professed openly, both were motivated by a declared admiration for the object: the analyst, the analytical function, the method, and the initial practice, which seemed to confirm the patient's very high expectations. Analysis is felt to be a beautiful healing process, that is, an intimate relationship which fosters unlimited freedom of thought, a free-dom that extends to the shadowy roots of anxiety which will be dispelled when exposed to the light of knowledge.

That said, a couple of questions arise: why was psychoanalysis neces-sary to restore the hope of a satisfactory and creative relationship with the object? And what lies behind this fervent admiration and imitative activ-ity? Obviously, there is the repeated narcissistic delusion regarding the impossible recovery and achievement of understanding with the primary object, which is caused by both the disproportionate nature of the impulse, and by the inescapable frustration that the object inflicts.

I should point out that the understanding of these cases of expansive appreciation of the object, which translated into an enthusiastic celebration of the bond between patient and analyst, and a powerful imitative desire, cannot be reduced to a simple split between an ideal and a persecutory object. To my mind it would be simplistic to interpret this imitative fer-vour as a mere defence against persecutory anxieties, and against the envy that the idealized object might induce. This would be to neglect sub-stantial aspects of the erotic – of the life drive, if one prefers this term – which is set in motion by the qualities inherent in the analytic frame and the attitude of the analyst. These are the qualities that actualize the broad spectrum of emotions and amorous feelings of the subject. It is the dis-covery of the good qualities of the object, and the subject's anxious need, that engenders hope-filled admiration, and its corollary, imitation.

When, during treatment, we try to understand the unconscious motiva-tions behind the imitative attitude, we think of the identificatory process and of the different types of identification. Is this observable practice of imitation the acting out of an unconscious phantasy which we refer to as projective identification? Or is it the result of a practice of projective identification, giving rise to an immersion, an emotional and cognitive coincidence with the object, and the recovery of the lost object via introjection?

Another alternative is to think that the imitative behaviour observed during treatment has to do with more primary processes of adhesion and mimesis, triggered not by recognition of the intrinsic qualities of the object being admired, but by the attempt to escape from the experience of annihilation and the despair arising from the subject's own inconsistency.

These questions can only be answered adequately from a genetic perspective that allows for a diachronic ordering of the imitative attitudes and their corresponding identificatory manifestations. We are helped in our understanding by infant observation studies, in conjunction with our experience of the infant rediscovered in regressive states which are actualized through transference. As that is not the main aim of this study, I shall limit myself to referring to E. Gaddini's review (1969) of the metapsychological level and, more recently, the work of D. Widlöcher (1986). With regard to the infant under observation, I also have in mind the reflections of D. Stern (1985) on the meaning and value of imitative behaviours on the part of young infant. It is not my intention, however, to offer a critical review, but rather merely to refer to the points which seem to me to be most pertinent to an understanding of imitative and hypocritical attitudes on the part of certain adult patients.

In his very succinct reflection on previous contributions, Gaddini describes imitation as a point of departure which, through the intermediate stage of introjection (internalization), ends up leading to full-blown identification. This is understood as assimilation, on the part of the self, of the qualities of the object. That said, this process is reversible; in other words, the identification or obstacles to identification can lead, via regression, to imitation.

Translating this to a clinical context, does the patient imitate us and imitate the spirit of the analytical method in order to finally consolidate a structuring identification? Or does the patient imitate us because they cannot identify with us? We are here alluding to the progressive and regressive value of imitation. Gaddini argues that what precedes precocious identification would be regarded as precocious imitation. This kind of imitation can be observed in the infant who is engaged in the most elemental conflict with the object. Then, the infant's perception of the object is itself perception-imitation. That is to say, it is movement which reproduces the object, and which at the same time grounds the identity of the subject. Therefore, and this is the essence of Gaddini's reflection, one can imitate in order to perceive, but one might also imitate in order to be, in order to construct an identity.

Lacan has exploited these aspects of imitation which lead eventually to identification in his theory building. He noted the paradoxical fact that we construct our identity by allying ourselves with a good containing object, but in the process lose ourselves as the subject. Far from becoming integrated and organized, the self is alienated through the flood of identifications it makes with the other.

We can find a critique of the Lacanian position in Widlöcher (1986), in his study *Identifier et s'identifier*. I cannot now detail the development of Lacan's theories, or Widlöcher's summary of these, but I will limit myself to highlighting those aspects most applicable to clinical practice. Especially useful are those which shed light, in accordance with the study of hysterical identification – Freud 1905 and 1921 – on the motivations and aims of observable imitative behaviours which raise questions about the nature of the imitated object. Is what is imitated the object of desire, or the object of the object of desire, or the ideal of the object?

I have already pointed out in passing that the enthusiastic and conscious imitative conduct of two patients demonstrated a direct imitation of the analyst, but often reflected, more or less precisely, a triangulation involving the patient, the analyst, and "psychoanalysis". The patient in both cases exhibited a "psychoanalytical" ideology and attitude, as if he were an analyst, in order to earn the appreciation of the analyst and to feel bonded with him in their love of the same profession.

It is, if you like, the application of what Freud (1921) studies in group dynamics – religious, military, etc. Freud notes that there is an identification with the leader, but also with all of the other members of the group, who all love the same idealized leader. In the situation of classical psychoanalytical treatment, the analyst is the leader, but they are also a peer, a fellow-admirer, along with the patient themselves, of the ideal psychoanalytical object.

Even though movement between the conscious, preconscious, and unconscious makes it difficult to clearly distinguish imitative conduct from its identificatory results, I feel it is relevant to highlight Julia Coromines's (1991, p. 114) insistence on the need to differentiate between imitation and archaic forms of adhesive identification. As she says, we need to "attribute to imitation intentionality, conscious action, which is not the case with adhesive identification".

5 Hypocrisy: between Self-deception and Fraud

Patients like B., after an initial effusive phase characterized by warm concurrence, evolved from extreme imitation towards a less enthusiastic attitude, persevering rather than fervent. B's perseverance during the course of treatment did not vacillate even amid painful experiences in the analysis of the transference. With variations arising from his particular psychopathology, his diligence remained strong despite the persistence of symptoms of negative character traits.

Outside the sessions, and in their professional spheres (they are often psychologists), these patients practise assistance or teaching related to psychoanalysis, follow psychoanalytical literature, attend seminars and courses and vigorously engage in discussion with colleagues from different schools of thought. This vibrant and decisive public outlook contrasts with the resigned stoicism that they exhibit in their own personal analytic sessions, where everything is less brilliant, and much more uncomfortable. This contrast produces perplexity in the analyst, as he or she has the persistent sense of a partial contact. Experiences which are not actualized in the sessions seem to be dramatized elsewhere. In any case, the analyst is left with the impression that the patient is disguised as an analyst, and that in the privacy of the sessions themselves they are wearied by the obstacles encountered during treatment, and by their own addiction to defensive mechanisms. They also complain about the exasperating wait for mutative interpretations.

In any case, the patient expresses his intention to fully assume the identity of analyst. In the sessions he tries hard to keep at bay any desire to fuse with the ideal object, with an all-powerful psychoanalysis, a fusion had seemed feasible during the now remote period of the analytical "honeymoon". He is clearly not a patient who lies, but he does conceal, even from himself, his longing for fusion. But, under the patient's stoical perseverance and his acceptance of the task of grieving, there lurks a dark fear of experiencing the forceful reappearance of the siren-song of psychoanalysis, replete with unlimited possibilities, from which he had expected so much. In the here-and-now of the sessions, the analyst does not tolerate well the embarrassed concealment of this spell-binding object of the patient's phantasy, which can hurt the therapist's self-esteem due to the paucity of results obtained from the process. If this situation goes unnoticed, countertransferential jealousy on the analyst's part, of which they are unaware, can induce rivalry with the patient's ideal object, which is hidden but whose presence is felt.

It is worth noting that these patients initially practise a conscious imitation of the analyst, and of the spirit of the method, motivated by their desire to become what they admire. Later they adopt a more hypocritical attitude, which they may recognize. This often evolves in a favourable direction, with a progressive acceptance that the analyst is not omnipotent. Is it possible to speak of a hypocrisy which remains enthusiastic, after the period of imitation and yearning for fusion has passed? Could we consider the need for a transitory coexistence with an object, felt to be ideal; an object which the analyst should continue to embody at the insistent demand of these patients?

This external attitude, recognized as hypocritical by the patient, and which causes them to suffer, reminds the analyst that this is not a lying patient, but someone who confronts the external manifestations of their own splitting, who owns them and brings them to the consulting room, without intuiting the reasons for their mental state.

Technical difficulties lie in the fact that the recognition of hypocrisy is not always so straightforward. Here also there is a broad spectrum of experiences and attitudes which persist in a nosological and structural continuity, ranging from a virtually oneiric mimetism in the form of an "as if" personality to mythomania, an entirely different kind of deliberate imitation that includes fraudulent lying, imposture, perverse and confusionary deception.

All these attitudes have clearly differentiated features, but these may merge in a complex fashion in the here and now of the sessions. What the analyst finds hardest to understand and tolerate is the deliberate intention to lie and deceive on the part of the patient, whatever the unconscious motives are that cause this behaviour. In the countertransference, what makes it particularly difficult for the analyst to remain benevolent is the mixture of truth and falsehood that the patient conveys.

E. O'Shaughnessy (1990) wonders whether it is possible to psychoanalyse a liar. Despite the difficulties, she opts for the viability – uncertain but possible – of the analytical process, provided attention is paid to a fundamental facet of the liar's mind, the clarification of which constitutes, undoubtedly, the most original aspect of the analyst's task. In fact, for O'Shaughnessy, the liar brings to analysis certain very primary problems which do not centre around the truth or falsehood of their statements, but rather around the truth or falsehood of their objects. As she points out at the end of her brilliant article, lying is associated with "doubts and anxieties on the liar's part in their communication with their primary objects, which, for a range of reasons have become, for him, lying objects".

As I have said, the patently hypocritical behaviour of the patients I am referring to is clearly different from that of the fraudulent liar. What does the hypocrite hide and dissimulate, and what does their hypocrisy denote? As in any symptomatic formation, something is always hidden. What I have been able to see in the evolution of different cases is that in the hypocritical behaviour displayed by patients in the sessions, they practised a self-pitying and playful submission in a so-called "servitude to the analysis", for the sake of a modest approximation to the difficult truth about themselves; a truth which they recognize as desirable and dreaded at the same time. The patient wishes to share these difficulties and invites us to participate in their stoicism and their scepticism.

The questions that arise concerning what is hidden and what appears on the surface are sometimes answered through dreams, and sometimes through phantasies or descriptions of their own experience as a therapist. And the counterweight to the attitude that comes across as fictitious is the growing conviction that the patient is hostage to a phantasy of an extraordinary and omnipotent psychoanalysis which is fresh and creative, in contrast to the arduous practice being pursued in the sessions. This aggrandized psychoanalysis of an often megalomaniac phantasy reminds us of the attitudes characterizing the initial, enthusiastic "honeymoon" period, as if the experience of participation in the ideal object had withdrawn in shame into a corner of the mind, but remained permeated with nostalgia and disappointment regarding the patient's possibilities; along with an artificial and hypocritical enthusiasm regarding the activity of the therapist or psychoanalyst.

In order to better understand hypocrisy, can O'Shaughnessy's theory be invoked to unravel the mystery of the internal relationship of the falsifier with his/their object?

I have successfully tested this theory in the countertransferential effervescence triggered by moments of stagnation or by particular recurring difficulties. By asking questions concerning the nature of the patient's object, as O'Shaughnessy and B. Joseph (1993) do, we might calmly hold at a distance the immediacy of the here and now, but to return to it later with fresh intuitions and possible verifications.

In any case, in the dynamic of hypocrisy, what is hidden is as important as what is exhibited. We wear disguises in order to appear as we are not, but we also disguise ourselves with what we would like to be. In every process of change, the identification conflict is present, with more or less turbulence, as in a pubertal or climacteric crisis, for example. In the course of the analytical process, the desired integration brought about by a reduction of splitting, the elaboration of grief and the repair of objects, is not linear but zig-zagged (remember the ante-chamber of the depressive condition as described by Meltzer). Just as in adolescence, there is a conflict between what one is and what one would like to become.

This situation is particularly tense in the case of patients who, in the course of treatment, are beginning their own practice of psychoanalytical psychotherapy, or have just started to interview their first patients. The ambiguity of the situation is not exclusively due to the fact of their adopting a new professional identity without definitive recognition from a psychoanalytical institution. There is a deeper issue, which lies in the conflictive coexistence of identifications: on the one hand, the adult part of the personality, with acceptance of one's own limitations and the slow reincorporation of projections; on the other hand, the gradual undermining of one's narcissistic organization, the frequent reappearances of which lead to triumphalism in the practice of psychoanalytical psychotherapy.

There are moments when the young candidate feels like Goldoni's hero, serving two masters: the infantile ideal self and the psychoanalytical object. They want to connect with the latter, to fully incorporate it once and for all; but they are still on a shorter pathway: that of omnipotence, of which they are sufficiently aware to want to hide it. As a patient, they are living behind the mask of an ideal of maturity; as a therapist, when real progress is being made, they end up identifying entirely with the mask; in other words, we are once again in the presence of the legend of the sanctified hypocrite.

6 Summary and Final Reflections

In the first place, my interest centred around the limits of truth and deception in the experience of being in love. The desire to conceal what is regarded as unacceptable in order to be loved led me to distinguish between a hypocritical behaviour deployed due to the predominance of the amorous impulse, and a hypocrisy governed by hate.

I have referred to patients with different psychopathologies, but who were both capable of maintaining a largely unconditional fervour towards the analyst, the analytical method and the possibilities offered by its practice. The aesthetic and ludic elements present at the beginning of treatment seem important for tolerating the conflicts and suffering awakened by it.

The analyst faces a delicate task if they want to avoid a double pitfall: on the one hand, a collusive idealization which seeks the chronic avoidance of conflict; on the other, the overhasty reduction of "transference love" and enthusiastic imitation to an ever-present defence mechanism. Between one pitfall and the other, what matters is to highlight the relationship between idealization and the patient's despair. The interpretation will be effective if it shows that the analyst tolerates both the idealization and that which the idealization is trying to conceal.

But, however good the technique, the disillusionment that must be accepted with respect to the initial expectations and the impossible re-idealization of the psychoanalytical object, lead to a continuation of the patient's enthusiastic desire to imitate. This is also driven by the patient's willingness to adapt to the new perspectives which the analyst has drawn attention to, the resulting renewed awareness and the demands that this entails. Despite this, it is clear that idealization persists, expressing itself in dreams or surreptitious behaviour. But in the last analysis, the adaptive façade is entirely unnecessary, because its disappearance coincides with genuine progress. I do not mean by this that such a positive outcome is the norm. Unfortunately, this hypocrisy can endure, and become toxic.

In these notes, on the basis of Freud's thesis concerning identification in an amorous relationship, I have applied a Kleinian understanding of the need for idealization so as to preserve the good object, and to protect oneself from the persecutory object. I have taken into account what Melanie Klein argues about the need for idealization in order for the good object to be repaired. Patients who make progress, like B., remind me of Klein's comments, in the same paper, concerning identification, when she refers to the structuring of the personality on the basis of the presence of a good internal object. Love of the good object "confers on the self a feeling of wealth and abundance ... the projection of the good parts of the *self* onto the external world will not entail feelings of impoverishment or emptiness ..." Though in the same passage of this paper on Identification, Klein states that

> as long as, in moments of gratification and love an undamaged breast is involved, this affects the way in which the self is split and projects. The feeling of preserving an intact nipple and breast, despite the

coexistence of phantasies of a breast being devoured bite by bite, results in the splitting and projection not being associated, mainly, with the fragmented parts of the personality, but with more coherent parts of the *self*.

(*The Writings of Melanie Klein*, III, p. 144)

I have referred to idealization in the service of creative outcomes, associated with the notion of libidinal narcissism as defended by M. Klein, Rosenfeld, and Gantheret, among others. I would now like to highlight an important difference between the hypocritical behaviours I have described and those studied by Alberto Campo, in which hypocrisy becomes an egosyntonic character trait. On the contrary, the hypocritical attitudes I have described, and their subsequently favourable evolution, are vicissitudes that are consciously in conflict with the rest of the self, often as a transient and shame-inducing recourse.

The legend of the sanctified hypocrite seems particularly significant in support of a conscious dichotomy between an attitude of undivided admiration for the good object and a hidden but consciously persisting attraction to a seductive object that is itself retreating. The hero of Julien Green's novel, *Si j'étais vous*, which Melanie Klein studies in her work on identification, does not identify out of love, but out of the need to assuage his emptiness, his destructiveness, and his envy, and to escape from himself and plunder the objects he invades. By contrast, Lord George is in love, and longs to become a saint in order to please a saint; he needs to assume the physiognomy of a saint, to immerse himself in it in order to be ultimately transformed into its identificatory shape. He is only a hypocrite in the sense that he hides his past history, and in this way, keeps at a distance a part of himself, the part that has to do with his past. However, his profession of love for the new object is by no means fictitious, but is full of enthusiasm. His self becomes solid enough to confront the despair of his past life.

A comparison between the protagonists of the stories of Julien Green and Max Beerbohm also invites us to contrast the character traits of the patients that I would place in the category of "sanctified hypocrite". One difference is the degree of consciousness displayed by the two characters: while Fabien, Green's hero, is in a coma and in this state develops his fantasies of successive intrusions into the lives of different people, Lord George is fully conscious of what he enthusiastically appears to be and of that which pleases his beloved, as well as of that which he strives to be rid of. My patients were also conscious of their imitative longing, of their enthusiasm for the admired object (the analyst, the analysis, etc.) and they were aware of the seductive power still being exercised by the old ideals of omnipotence. This was an awareness which disrupted what might otherwise have been an evolution towards a depressive state.

As I have pointed out in this paper, I do not wish to fall into a naïve optimism concerning the severity of certain structures with their inveterate equilibria resulting from rigid cleavages. Concurring with Victor Hernandez, I am convinced that it would take a saint to bring about maturity in certain perverse organizations of the personality. But the story of the *Happy Hypocrite* reminds us of something which, at certain moments of the countertransferential experience, we might have left to one side. That is, that the relationship with the good object might have been drastically split, and the patient might require an actual experience, such as an analysis, to enable them to bring back to life the good object and, on that basis, the reorganization of their self. While this change is still underway, we analysts should tolerate the temporary organization on the part of the patient who is denying less and less their narcissistic wound, even while they try to conceal, with embarrassment and even hypocrisy, the scars that it has left.

Note

1 Published in *Revista Catalana de Psicoanàlisi*, vol. XI, nos 1–2, 1994.

Bibliography

Beerbohm, M. (1970) The happy hypocrite, in *The Bodley Head Selection*, London.

Bion, W. R. (1970) *Attention and Interpretation*, Tavistock Publications, London.

Campo, A. J. (1967) La hipocresía como trastorno del carácter. Dificultades técnicas que plantea en relación con la asociación libre. *Revista de Psicoanálisis*, vol. 24 , no. 3.

Coromines, J. (1991) *Psicopatologia i desenvolupament arcaics*, Espax, Barcelona.

Freud, S. (1905) Fragment of an analysis of a case of hysteria. *The Standard Edition of the Complete Psychological Works of Sigmund Freud*, vol. VII.

Freud, S. (1910) Five Lectures on Psychoanalysis. *The Standard Edition of the Complete Psychological Works of Sigmund Freud*, vol. XI.

Freud, S. (1914) On Narcissism: An Introduction. *The Standard Edition of the Complete Psychological Works of Sigmund Freud*, vol. XIV.

Freud, S. (1921) Group psychology and the analysis of the ego. *The Standard Edition of the Complete Works of Sigmund Freud*, vol. XVIII.

Gaddini, E. (1969) On imitation, *Int. Journal of Psycho-Anal*, vol. 50, no. 4.

Gantheret, F. (1990) *El narcisisme en l'obra de Rainer Maria Rilke, in Psicoanàlisi i Literatura-Implicacions recíproques*, Fundació Caixa de Pensions, Barcelona.

Hernández, V. (1993) Personal communication at the Institute of Psychoanalysis, Barcelona.

Joseph, B. (1993) Summary of the paper "Hearing and experiencing in the treatment of child and adult patients", *Psychoanalysis in Europe*, Bulletin 40.

Klein, M. (1946) Notes on some schizoid mechanisms, in *The Writings of M. Klein*, vol. III.

Klein, M. (1952) On observing the behaviour of young infants, in *The Writings of M. Klein*, vol. III.

Klein, M. (1955) On identification, in *The Writings of M. Klein*, vol. III.

Klein, M. (1957) Envy and gratitude, in *The Writings of M. Klein*, vol. III.

Meltzer, D. (1967) *The Psychoanalytical Process*, Heinemann, London.

O'Shaughnessy, E. (1990) Can a liar be psychoanalysed? *Int. Journal of Psycho-Anal*, vol. 71, no. 2.

Stern, D. N. (1985) *The Interpersonal World of the Infant*. Basic Books, New York.

Widlöcher, D. (1986) Identifier et s'identifier, in *Métapsychologie du sens*, PUF, Paris.

6 Particularities of the Musical Symbol[1]

Pere Folch Mateu

1 Introduction

In recent years, music and psychoanalysis have been forging more and more links. A large number of psychoanalytic works refer to the connections between the two fields, as if psychoanalysts wished to respond to Freud's purported indifference to music. But, even if Freud said he was *ganz unmusikalisch*, totally unmusical, or that he had no gift for music, there's no doubt that persistent Freudian research into the meaning and sense of music is what encourages today's psychoanalysts to explore so many questions about its enigmatic, penetrating impact.

In any case, this growing interest in music could be related to a similar burgeoning interest among psychoanalysts in the phenomena of conduct as well as in very primitive forms of communication. Freud, in an early period to which he remained more or less faithful, thought that any investigation of the unconscious had to be carried out by way of verbal language. In his view, access to meaning, or to any thing lying beyond the manifest elements of experience, could only be gained through the medium of the word. But psychoanalysis has developed in different directions, in terms of both theory and technique. Clinical experience with very small children or with seriously ill patients has convinced us that a capacity for symbolization develops long before verbal language does. The infant's first representations aren't verbal. They stem from primary emotional experiences that are felt amid a range of sensations: tactile, olfactory, kinetic, visceral and, very soon, acoustic, in noises and sounds. All these appreciable signs keep acquiring semantic value which depends on such elementary factors as frequency, tonal variation, changing rhythms, bursts of sound, and silences. All of this is highlighted by research into the infant's preverbal life by Daniel N. Stern (1985) and many other scholars in the field of evolutionary psychology.

The psychoanalyst must be able to notice the expressive richness of all these preverbal signs and symbols in order to understand and enter into contact with an autistic or psychotic child. In other words, it is necessary to become familiar with this primitive language: a visceral, sensorial, emotional language which hasn't yet acquired semantic precision.

DOI: 10.4324/9781003342472-6

Early psychoanalytic treatment of such serious cases has corresponded with systematic research into the earliest periods of psychic life and, in particular, the first six months of life. It must be said that delving into these early stages of the life of relations and of intrapsychic life – what the baby perceives, expresses, and thinks – has been an extraordinary help in understanding adults. Now we more accurately capture the value of the paraverbal and extraverbal elements of language. We have learned to assess more precisely, outside of lexical content and verbal style, the prosodic elements of language. To sum up, it is through the musical elements of language – rhythm, tone, cadence, silence, and so on – that we manage to make contact with our patients' deepest emotions. What the word can't say, or what the word can't unconsciously hide, disguise, or repress, comes to us in a more direct form through all these elements that surround lexemes.

2 The Expressive and Communicative Possibilities of Music: the Signifier and the Signified in the Structure of the Musical Symbol

It is very strange to see the widely differing views on the expressive possibilities of music and also concerning the precision or ambiguity of musical semantics. In his work *Emotion and Meaning in Music*, Leonard Meyer remarks on these differences and separates the theorists into two main groups. First, there are the absolutists who think that the meaning of music lies exclusively in the context of the work, and in perception of the links therein. Second, there are the referentialists who hold that besides this abstract meaning, music conveys other meanings that derive from the extra-musical world of concepts, actions, and emotional states. As Anthony Storr (1992) explains, the contrasting views of composers and musicologists can be related to those of many other writers, some of whom argue in favour of the greater concision of the musical message. Paul Valéry, for example, said that the instruments of music are much more precise than those of writing. Sounds can be rigorously delimited in their value while the word, the tool of the poets, is an instrument of maddening ambiguity. Mendelssohn, too, thought that music is less ambiguous than verbal language, and Proust went so far as to say that the future of humanity, or of understanding amongst human beings, would be very different if we communicated using music rather than with spoken language.

I don't know what musicians think about these possible, as yet unfulfilled possibilities of communication without the impediments of verbal language, because musicians, like the rest of us, are immersed in this universe of verbal thought. In any case, the only way they have of expressing, in any understandable way, what they are trying to communicate through their musical language, is by means of concepts and words. It should be said that, when it comes to interpreting music, language hasn't performed very well, even when musicians are the ones attempting to do it. As Roland Barthes says, this becomes clear in musical criticism where often, "it can readily be seen that a work (or its performance) is only ever translated into the poorest of linguistic categories: the adjective" which, in fact, offers little information.

I hope that, in our debate, we can discuss this supposed discrediting of the word, this inadequacy of the word for the communication of intimate experience and, in particular, the most basic emotional experiences. The deficiency of verbal language has been robustly pointed out by writers like Victor Zuckerkandl, who is quoted by Anthony Storr. Zuckerkandl, whose work on the conundrum of the musical symbol has mostly been seen in the volumes of *Sound and Symbol* and is also expressed in his essay "The Sense of Music", starts out from the otherwise highly contentious hypothesis that the word would constantly break up the unity of existence, separating one thing from another and dividing subject from object. Tone, by contrast, would restore this unity. Music would save the world from being totally transformed in language; would prevent it from becoming pure object, and would save man from becoming pure subject.

The contradiction sometimes expressed by musicians in this debate about the intrinsic or referential meaning of a musical work is also curious. Some, like Stravinsky, claim that their art of composition is pure engineering, a sonic construction that makes no attempt to represent anything but itself. They are therefore situated a long way from any emotional motivation which, others would say, might have prompted them to compose. But Stravinsky himself, demonstrating his intellectual mettle, also declared that the motivation that sometimes drove him to compose came in the form of a dream. One can see this in the oneiric experience of complex sensuality and fantasy that emerge in the first bars of his *Rite of Spring*. Stravinsky said, "I heard and I wrote what I heard. I am the vessel through which *Le Sacré* passed".

For other composers, the starting point has been the wish to represent sounds captured in the flow of conscious experience, a representation that ultimately finds a container in musical production. There are other times when composers say that they find the sound not in any mental representation but through finding it materially on the piano. Finally, taking a reverse path, still other composers explain that it all begins with a pencil and paper, in writing a note or a series of notes. It is then this writing that gives rise to a sound. Hence, in some cases, the beginning of a composition is a mental representation of sounds and, in others, the representation in writing is the start of the composition.

However, I won't continue along this track as I think it's up to musicians to illustrate for us the different ways in which the musical symbol is generated in the composer's creative process. The Catalan composer and musical theorist Josep Soler has spoken at length, pertinently, about the intimate and dramatic motivation for the transformation of emotional experience into the musical score. Indeed, it is largely thanks to Soler that I have come to understand the vicissitudes of the process of transformation of emotional experience into a score.

If I have dwelt on these points here, it has been in order to situate part of the discussion about this much-debated question of the structure of the musical symbol and the link between the signifier and the signified. Even if only schematically, I'd like to comment that the notion that music is nothing more than a kind of logic, albeit one that is beautifully constructed as an arrangement of sounds, seems implausible to me. I am in total agreement with Susan Langer, however, when she suggests that there can be no aesthetic value without meaning or, putting it more strongly, that the aesthetic value of a work is conferred by its signifying power.

Yet, musical signifying is very different from that of discursive symbols, which again contrast with Langer's presentational symbols, amongst which music must be included. The meaning and sense of music wouldn't be found in a denotation of what is signified but in a connotation. To conclude this point, I'll add that the link between signifier and signified in music is unconscious, as is the creative process itself. Artists and composers try to explain, in *a posteriori* introspection, what has taken place within them, but the only thing they can say is that their work is a more or less inspired construction. They sound rather like someone trying to talk about a vague dream. The dream experience can be transformed into verbal discourse, but that which has produced the dream, the unconscious emotional experience that generates it, remains ineffable. About this experience, we can only make more or less convincing inferences.

3 Musical Elements of Preverbal Communication and Musical Elements of Verbal Language: Vital Sentiments and Categorical Sentiments

Acoustic stimuli, together with kinetics, are the oldest features of the infant's perceptive and emotional life. Intrauterine life is dominated by two rhythmic sounds: the mother's heartbeat, and the baby's own heartbeat. These rhythms are modified in intensity and frequency with the mother's physical exercise and by the toxic effects deriving from the food she eats. They are also disturbed by emotion, such as by the weight of emotion conveyed in the mother's breath. The heartbeat becomes faster or slower, makes tiny stops, and is characterized by an intensity that fluctuates with activity and repose. There is a very clear interaction between the vital signs of mother and baby. One can't talk about a union between mother and baby in the most literal sense of the term, as in two hearts in unison, but it is possible to speak of a communication that is very elementary and not reducible to the connection provided by umbilical and placental circulation. While still in the womb, the child starts to become differentiated as a subject, and establishes the first vague notions of inside and outside, pleasure and unpleasure and closeness and distance, the precision of which is honed thanks to auditory stimuli. Once outside the womb, in the first hours of life, auditory stimuli very precociously affect the child, who is very soon able to single out the mother's voice from that of any other. Above all, it is the timbre of her voice and the melody of her language that captivate the baby. If the mother speaks without intonation, as if reading a paragraph backwards, the baby ceases to respond.

When other sensations – visual, kinaesthetic or kinetic, for example – are still diffuse and imprecise, the mother's verbal rhythms, her prosody and the modulations of her intonation, quickly favour her recognition by the infant. There is a growing understanding of the messages conveyed by her, through variations in the intensity, tone, and beat of her verbal sequence, with accelerations or slowing down of the verbal flow, with sudden or predictable silences, and with repeated guttural sounds, words, laughter, and murmurs. In other words, the infant comes to know the whole range of vocal variations lavished by the mother in this early stage of his life. In these beginnings, language is practically an array of sounds and noises, a gestural complexity that will acquire semantic precision in a surprisingly short period of time.

The capacity of infants for perceptive evolution in the first year is truly impressive, and it is even more surprising when our observations verify their innate functional state. To put it briefly and clearly, in its first three months of life, the baby is capable of making abstract representations of his experience of perception. These abstract representations don't pertain to things seen or touched but, rather, to forms, intensities, temporal models, rhythms, bursts of sound, variations of intensity and beat, and qualities of suffering. This is what Daniel Stern conceptualizes as "vitality affects", or forms of feeling that are closely linked with the processes of life. Later, but still at a very early stage of evolution, the infant is able to exercise physiognomic perception, and the affects involved in this are more nuanced: sadness, irritation, rage, and joy. Stern calls these categorical affects.

Both visual and categorical affects have the particularity of being experienced by the infant in a type of perception that psychologists call amodal perception. This means that the child acquires information received in a sensorial modality and moves it into another sensorial modality. Infants recognize that what they see, hear, and touch, all belong to the same object. This transposition from one perceptive channel to another enriches the infant's sense of the object and this sense becomes a literal "common sense" as Bion (1963) puts it. Somehow, the metaphorical capacity of the adult, enhancer of the meaning of language, uses the transposition and transformation of one sensorial impression into another. Hence, music is, for some, an impetus, or pure kinetic pleasure, but for others, like the philosopher Eugenio Trías (1991), it is an architecture, a sonic building, a retreat. In the first of his "Sonnets to Orpheus", Rilke (1922) speaks of transformed music. Orpheus sings and plays his lyre and creates a "great tree of sound". In the last verse of the sonnet, speaking of the animals that come to listen, he says, "You have fashioned them a temple for their hearing". This idea of the ambit, the container, the building that music creates, led Eugenio Trías to bring music and architecture together in a brilliant, suggestive elaboration of the poetic metaphor.

4 Musical Experience, Object Relations and Transference: the Psychology of the Listener, Archaic Object Relations, and the Relation with the Musical Object

Listening to a musical composition arouses in the listener a varying range of affects, feelings, memories, and fantasies that are different, from subject to subject, independent of the composer's intentions. What happens in this evocative process of listening to a musical work? The psychoanalyst tries to explain the listener's relationship with music according to the pattern of his object relations. That is to say, it is a relationship characterized by an interaction between two parties. Hence, in language, it is expressed as an exchange, a movement of a person's own aspects projected into the musical object and an introjection of aspects of this very particular object such as a melody or a sonata. The process is mostly unconscious. The moments that become present for us belong to part of this cycle of movement that goes from us into the musical work, and from it, in to us.

I believe that, like any aesthetic experience, the musical work awakens a complex transferential process. Music saddens, gives happiness, creates imaginary scenes, and awakens particular memories. Music is a particularly apt continent where listeners can project their individual internal situations which are mobilized by listening.

Transference, a concept formulated by psychoanalysts, refers to an important component of the patient's relation to the analyst. Transference means transport and, in the analytic situation, it refers to the transport of aspects of the patient's past and inner world, and of all kinds of drives and feelings into the present of his relationship with the psychoanalyst. In fact, this process is a universal phenomenon particular to human relations, and it is equally appropriate to apply it to the relationship that is established between the spectator and a work of art.

To clarify this, I'll explain this recurrent transference with reference to what a musician, Hindemith, and a poet, Rilke, have to say. Neither of them calls the phenomenon by the name with which psychoanalysts have baptized it, but each gives a vivid description of the process which psychoanalysts contemplate and deal with in their patients on a daily basis.

In his book *A Composer's World*, Paul Hindemith (1961) speaks sceptically about what music can convey of the composer's feelings. He says rather that the musician knows from experience that certain sets of tones match certain emotional reactions of the listener. He stresses this point, saying that music is not about expressing universal or personal emotions: "[The] emotions released by music are not real emotions, they are mere images of emotion that have been experienced before [...] and not the real, untransformed, and unmodified feelings". They are the images or memories of music, and whilst the listener believes he or she is being moved by the music, he or she is in fact transporting or transferring to the music emotions and images of his or her own experience. Hindemith is describing the transferential process. The patient, too, feels he is in love with the analyst, or has aggressive fantasies towards her but is unaware that he is transporting, or transferring to her feelings from another time, emotions that have remained anchored within him, and that he brings into his relation to the analyst as part of an unconscious process. Hindemith would say that these emotions *vis-à-vis* the analyst aren't real emotions. What happens is that the therapeutic situation is appropriate for arousing this transport or transference of the most intimate and most archaic drives, emotions, and feelings of the patient's life. The patient may believe that his feelings can be explained only by the presence of the therapist, but this is because he is unaware of the unconscious process which makes him project what he bears inside into the figure of the analyst. Music could also be such a transference object, provoking as it does the projection of an emotional atmosphere into the musical work. Like the analyst in the clinical situation, the musical work would only be the medium for updating and transferring very intimate aspects of the deepest unconscious of the sensitive listener.

This inner world that is expressed in the relationship with the analyst and in the atmosphere created by music is expressed poetically by Rainer Maria Rilke, who speaks of music as "the transformation // of feelings into what? – Into audible landscape". Rilke continues with the theme of this externalization of a deepest intimacy a few lines below: "holy departure: // when the innermost point in us stands // outside, as the most practised distance ..." As far as I know, the transferential movement has never been expressed so vigorously and so beautifully. It is a way of finding outside ourselves the deepest depths of our experience. Music would be the occasion of meeting this familiar distance, or the unconscious. It offers itself as a means of making the internal external, and thus for rediscovering as many intimacies as are projected.

It has therefore been possible to say that music is a transitional object, like those objects described by psychoanalysts, and especially by Winnicott (1971). Such an object is one which the child feels to be of mixed quality: partly belonging to himself, and partly recognized as being external to himself. It belongs to the period of only partial subject–object differentiation, when the infant still hasn't accepted separation from the mother and bonds with material objects (dummy, pillows, certain toys like teddy bears, and so on) that stand for her. The child projects a good part of his fantasy into these objects, especially his image of the mother, who thereby becomes controlled as if she were a material thing, within reach and able to vividly evoke what is missing. But this mixed quality of the absent object and present object can be experienced not only in relation to tangible objects or things. A murmur, a lullaby, or a guttural sound can also have this function of an intermediary object.

At this point I'd like to highlight what the psychoanalyst and musician Ludwig Haesler (1992) drew attention to in a recent article. He refers to the use of sensorial, acoustic phenomena in representing the absent object, and makes a comparison between the semantic, dynamic, and formal structures inherent in music. For him, music can acquire the specific function of a transitional object which, because of its particular acoustic qualities and its structure, comes, in an illusory space, to represent the missing object.

5 The Listener's Anxieties and Defences

If a piece of music has this ability to become a meeting point between the internal and external world in the listener's mind, this may be because of the qualities of musical composition I have mentioned above, among which are archaic, preverbal elements of human communication. These are the elements – rhythms, intensities, bursts and fading away of sound, crescendos and diminuendos – that facilitate an evocation of the stage of subject–object non-differentiation. I'd also say that the listener, affected by these qualities of the music and its potential for evocation, is immersed in a kind of multivocal experience. Nothing guarantees that the generation of emotions will happen placidly. On the contrary, as we'll see below, the musical experience can have a vastly different impact depending on the particular interlacing of aesthetic pleasure and anxiety it evokes.

This brings us to the problem of the listener's resistance to music as a way of escaping the different emotions it may bring about. This resistance could be expressed in many ways, among them in an uneasiness, in a denial of the message, in boredom, and in distraction. Although this is of more interest to the psychologist than to the composer, the musical educator should bear in mind the emotional difficulties that may be encountered in any reception of a musical message. Such understanding may favour, as it could in a psychoanalytic treatment, the dissolution of these resistances.

6 Final Remarks and Consultation with the Musician

I have offered this brief overview of some of the problems arising when we consider the function and symbolic structure of music with the main aim of setting up a discussion and ongoing exchange between the musician, the psychoanalyst, and the aesthete. For psychoanalysts who work to interpret the unconscious and to understand its translation, via transference, into drama or dialogue, there would be no doubt about the benefit of this exchange. Indeed, one way of entering into contact with one's most intimate parts is by engaging in a dramatization of this interiority in the analyst–analysand relationship.

By contrast, the artist is able to bring out the unconscious, to organize and shape it by transforming the most primary emotional experiences into poetry, physical art, or music. The process of transformation of music in the mind is in turn fascinating for the psychoanalyst, especially because in shaping the musical symbol, the composer uses more distant, abstract elements, less concrete, sensorial, or kinetic. The conjunctive power of the symbol is confirmed in the tense relationship between signifier and signified. In his recent contribution to these debates, Glyn Morrill (1993) reminds us of this when he refers to the tension that exists between a logical sense and another meaning. I wonder if we could apply to music what he and Anna Gavarró have suggested in the case of verbal language, when they say that if the signs of natural language are sounds, when they become music, "they have become symbol with their evolutionary power as sense". As Morrill says, "one semiotic system is constructed on the basis of another". Music has the ineffable virtue of agreeing to and containing in the construction of its sonorous building (the "temple in the ear", as Rilke put it) the most elemental expressive categories (tempo, beat, fluctuations of vitality, etc.) and more elaborated and abstract thought.

The dynamics of the creative process in the mind of the musician make one think of something that interests the psychologist, namely the universal process of transformation of the most primary emotional experiences into meaningful symbolic and communicable formations. By contrast, the listener is interested in both the composer and the performer. This is what I wanted to approach succinctly when speaking about the relationship of the listener with the musical work as one with a propensity for creating pleasure, opening up ways of thought, and causing anxiety.

So, what are the anxieties that listening to music, as a whole aesthetic experience, can awaken? The psychoanalyst tends to detect anxiety in its most conscious forms, as a present experience, but most of all in the form in which it is denied. That is to say, the analyst sees anxiety in the various defences that are also manifest in listening to music. With this, we come to the listener's pathology, and I think the musician can't be indifferent to this. From rejection of new music, to the fetishistic degradation of music that Ludwig Haesler discusses, through to a use of music that is purely aimed at exciting sensoriality and sexuality, there are a whole range of defensive manifestations against the anxiety brought on by music.

There are some listeners, for example, who become anxious or consciously uneasy because they can't find any meaning in what they are listening to. They try to discover the meaning by seeking literary enlightenment, for example in a biography of the composer. In his master classes given in

Vienna (1932–1933), Webern recalled this when speaking of certain people who listen to music but don't feel calm unless it can represent a green field, a babbling brook, or a cuckoo singing, as if everyone needs music to express what they already know. "There must have been a need, some underlying necessity, for what we call music to have arisen. What necessity? To say something, express something, to express an idea that can't be expressed in any way but sound." Other listeners defend themselves from the anxiety caused by the abstract impact of the musical work by getting bored, distracted, and transforming listening into the creation of background music for fantasy, the anecdotal character of which contrasts with the musical semantic imprecision of the work.

There are, however, listeners with enough sensitivity and reflexive intuition to be able to communicate the unease stirred up by music that doesn't come with the precision of the word. They tell us that they are disturbed by the immersion in moods, internal climates or states of mind, without precise contents. Such experiences are therefore huge and easy to get lost in; they embody death and life, or presence and absence.

Evidently, we can't say everything in this first meeting with musicians. There are still a whole series of questions they might be able to answer. What do they think about experimentation with listeners to ascertain the debated musical semantics conveyed by some or other musical style? What do they think about the inductive power of music and its application to musical therapy today? What would be an appropriate approach to experimentation that could inform us not only about the psychology of the listener but also about the meaningful power of the work?

I shall now end where I should have begun, by thanking everyone who has helped me with the presentation of this psychoanalytic consultation addressed to musicians: first, my gratitude to the receptive sensibility and didactic capacity, full of patience and humour, of Josep Soler; to Petri Palou for the continued help and guidance with information she has given me for such a long time; to Anna Duran, who has updated me about present praxis in musicotherapy; and to other musicians – composers and performers – who have always been so willing to share these issues that music and psychoanalysis have the occasion to approach and re-approach.

Note

1 In P. Folch and M. T. Miró, eds (1995) *Debats a la cruïlla sobre el símbol*, Promociones y Publicaciones Universitarias, Barcelona.

Bibliography

Bion, W. (1963) *Elements of Psycho-Analysis*, Heinemann, London.
Caïn, J. *et al.* (1982) Freud, 'absolutement pas musicien'..., in *Psychanalyse et Musique*, Societé d'Édiction Les Belles Lettres-Paris.

Haesler, L. (1992) Music as a transitional object, *British Psychoanalytical Society Bulletin*, Vol. 28, N° 7.

Hindemith, P. (1961) *A Composer's World*, Anchor Books, New York.

Langer, S. K. (1956) *Philosophy in a New Key*, Harvard University Press, Cambridge MA. (1979).

Meyer, L. B. (1956) *Emotion and Meaning in Music*, University of Chicago Press.

Morrill, G. and Gavarró. A. (1993) Semiòtica, funció simbòlica i llenguatge poètic, in P. Folch and M. T. Miró (eds) (1995) *Debats a la cruilla sobre el símbol*, Promociones y Publicaciones Universitarias, Barcelona, pp. 169–175.

Rilke, R. M. (1918) An die Musik, in *Rilke Werke*, vol. 2, p. 111, Suhrkamp Verlag (1991).

Rilke, R. M. (1922) *Die Sonette an Orpheus*, Vol. 1, pp. 483–526.

Soler, J. (1982) Sobre la estructura del acto creador en música, *Revista de Musicología*, vol. V, no. 1.

Stern, D. N. (1985) *The Interpersonal World of the Infant*, Basic Books, New York.

Storr, A. (1992) *Music and the Mind*, HarperCollins.

Stravinsky, I. (1947) *Poética musical*, Taurus (1981); in English (1970): *Poetics of Music in the Form of Six Lessons*, Harvard University Press, Cambridge MA.

Stravinsky, I. and Craft, R. (1962) *Expositions and Developments*, Faber & Faber, London.

Trías, E. (1991) *Lógica del límite*, Ed. Destino, S.A.

Webern, A (1932–1933) *El cami cap a la nova música*, Antoni Basch, ed. (1982); in English (1963): *The Path to the New Music*, Theodor Presser Company, online at: https://archive.org/stream/antonwebernthepa007300mbp/antonwebernthepa007300mbp_djvu.txt

Winnicott, D. W. (1971) *Playing and Reality*, Tavistock Publications, London.

7 In Homage to Bion

The Theoretical and Clinical Validity of His Thought[1]

Pere Folch Mateu

Binocular Vision: Groupality and the Subject

A homage includes admiration for and gratitude to a man and his work: admiration for his innovative creative capacity and for the beauty of his message. It constitutes recognition when what we admire has become gradually inscribed in our praxis, making our task easier both with regard to patients and in terms of our ability to understand our experience with them in the course of the therapeutic process.

Many of us are affected by, if not imbued with Bion's thinking, though we have incorporated and elaborated it differently, to greater or lesser degrees, and with preferences and omissions in the leitmotifs of his teaching. The aim of this panel session is to present some of our favourite points of Bion's magnum opus, to comment on the use we've been able to make of them, and to see if we're able to take this use further by developing what is already prefigured in Bion's creative work.

The matter I'd like to talk about today is contained and condensed, as so many of Bion's ideas are, in the apparent simplicity of a metaphor, namely that of *binocular vision*. A concept pertaining to both technical and theoretical dimensions, it is an aid for practising and developing a better proliferation of the contents of experience, both inside and outside of the session.

The practice of adopting binocular vision can't be carried out as a voluntary act. We can't deliberately set about thinking and feeling from two more or less opposed mental positions. However, if we situate ourselves before the patient in the state of mind that Bion recommends, without memory or desire, we nurture mobility of emotion and thought, and their confluence from more or less distant provinces of the internal world. This confluence is highly improbable when memory and desire select and, so to say, make the mind focus in specific directions.

This binocular vision entails the conjugation of two vertices of the same experience. Perhaps the most elemental form of this conjugation is the convergence of external reality and internal reality; the meeting point of inside and outside, of what we perceive of external reality and of what we

DOI: 10.4324/9781003342472-7

feel emerging within ourselves in the form of appetite, rejection, satisfaction or fear. The perceived qualities of the external world are so impregnated with the intrinsic qualities of the person who captures them, that it could be said that external and internal reality are reciprocally mirrored. Thus, in order to express itself, an emotion coming up from within must find a sensorial garb to signify it and, on the contrary, a perceptive or sensorial impact must link up with the inner world if it is to acquire sense.

In the clinical situation, this is expressed by saying that an emotion or unconscious phantasy can only be experienced when connected to an external reality. Correspondingly, knowledge or understanding of what a patient says to us can only be gleaned if observation of what he says and does is combined with the resonance it finds within us, in the particular quality of the emotion it awakens.

This paradox, that internality must be known through its transferential conjugation with external reality, and that external reality must be known by looking within or feeling the resonance it finds inside us, has found different expressions in psychoanalysis. This fecund meeting point between outside and inside, between unconscious psychic reality and the world of consciousness-perception has been assigned to the area which, since Freud, we have called *preconscious* and which Bion, in his own conceptualization, has described as an *alpha screen*, a contact barrier between conscious and unconscious. This barrier not only distinguishes the two, but allows each to be related to separately, since the barrier between them is maintained without the other being dispersed. Thus, contact is maintained with both. We might say that the alpha screen ensures an optimal distance between the conscious and unconscious, so that the inside world and the outside world are reciprocally signified. The result of the *binocular vision*, of this correlation between inside and outside, comes quite close to the conditions for symbol formation, which also requires an optimal distance between objects, where one object stands for another.

The metaphor of *binocular vision*, which is so linked with that of *multiple vertices*, may be applied to phenomena as elemental as recognition of an object perceived through two or more perceptive channels. Thus, different senses together provide a "shared sense", which was the original meaning of the term "common sense". The metaphor is also applied to complex clinical situations. In effect, the experience the psychoanalyst has of the session is the result of his or her dual role as participant and observer. Participation and observation would be the two vertices by means of which a binocular vision of the relational situation with the patient obtains.

The use of binocular vision for facilitating the cognitive possibilities of an experience acknowledges the geographic or spatial aspects of two points of view, as well as the unconscious quality of the two vertices, as happens with a concrete optical image which is actually composed of right and left visual perception. Just as the single visual image doesn't enable one to decipher its components, namely the partial images of the right eye and the left eye, so the representation of an experience does not allow for a deciphering of the exogenous, perceptual elements, as distinct from the endogenous emotional elements that have come together in the singular rendering of the representation.

The model or metaphor of binocular vision pertains to a clinical and technical reality which the psychoanalyst experiences, and out of which he forms a representation. It is evident that this representation depends both on the convergent vision of more than one point of view and, in the negative sense, the splitting that disrupts the production of that convergence.

With this brief presentation I'd like to point out another, perhaps imperative connection necessitating the use of binocular vision: the link between the group therapeutic experience and the individual therapeutic experience, between the group mind and the individual mind, between the gregarious-group sector and the individual sector of the personality and, if we're not scared of neologisms, between *groupality* and *subjectality*.

The practice of group analytical psychotherapy, according to Bion's guidelines of understanding the movements of the group as a whole, has allowed a deepening in understanding of the dynamics of the individual mind. The two practices – individual analysis and group analysis – have complemented one another and, I believe, have reciprocally influenced one another. In particular, those psychoanalysts who have worked with both methods, have been able to confirm correspondences between the arduous coexistence of the members of the group and the often difficult coexistence in the individual patient of the self and its objects. In treatment, these facets are transformed into differentiated transferential updates which are, at times, difficult to link up; a situation that makes for a not very unitary psychic functioning at times, even if at others, the subject feels himself to be relatively well integrated.

Then again, the clinical movements of the group, carried out by several individuals who meet in the group therapy setting, happen in keeping with a dynamic which required Bion's brilliance and genius to make it understandable. It was Bion who showed us that the way of understanding a concurrence of eight or ten people was to conceive of them as forming a set, a singular entity – the group – which functions like a mind that is little or highly differentiated in terms of objects and functions. Among these, movements are established which are comparable to those we understand as influencing the coming into being of an individual mind.

When engaged in studying the group, Bion discovered in the clinical movement of group analytic sessions a particular kind of interaction among group members that evoked virtual intrapsychic movements between different parts of the self and the individual patient's internal objects. If the individual patient is understood as an intrapsychic plurality in conflict, then the plurality of individuals in a group is also understood as a mythical individuality that confronts conflicts and anxieties with particular defensive patterns, and a whole repertoire of basic assumptions.

I won't go into further technical details here. It is enough to point out this particular correspondence or correlation between the plurality of the individual's mind and that of the group, the coming into being of which is shaped in the setting and with the technique of group analysis. Bion makes us see the contrast between these two orders of experience: (a) that of the individual inserted into the dynamics of a group; and (b) the group or tribal characteristics of the individual mind.

The group shows, in its functioning, some elements or members that interact, blending together, dispersing, or attacking each other, moved by cataclysmic anxieties of fragmentation, confusion, and derealization. These anxieties demand more and more responses and defensive organizations, which Bion described as the group's basic assumptions. However, as in the mind of psychotic, these defences may become as problematic as the anxieties that produce them, which is why basic assumptions are rarely successful and tend to recur in repetitive cycles. Nevertheless, the group isn't drained by this elementality but is able, in a satisfactory evolution, to function on the basis of cooperation among the individuals that comprise it.

In pointing out the distinction between the basic assumption group and the work group, Bion (1952) calls attention to a differentiation in the group which is not unlike the one he would establish some years later (1957) between the psychotic and non-psychotic parts of the personality. The basic assumption group would coincide in many ways with the psychotic mind. By contrast, the work group can function in accordance with the structural model of the mature mind, the individuality of which rests on a broad interchange of its different elements (different parts of the self and internal objects), when there predominates among them a regime of differentiation and of freedom of assembly (Klein 1958).

Continued research in individual psychoanalysis, group analysis, the analysis of very small children, the systematic observation of babies, the treatment of autistic children, and into prenatal and postnatal studies, might have led Bion to ponder a proto-mental or somato-psychotic life. This referred to the very incipient forms of mental life which exist prior to symbolization and the emergence of meaningful thought. Such forms are closer to tropisms and valences than to a clear representation and recognition of the object and the self. For Bion, this was a state close to certain aspects of Freud's state of primary narcissism.

These aspects of proto-mental life, which are so linked to perinatal experiences and the uncertainties of the discovery of the object, would not fit with the requirements and vicissitudes of individuation. Intolerance of recognizing one's individual predicament, of existential solitude, and of the conflict of otherness, could lead the individual to take shelter in the gregarious life, and to adapt to patterns dictated by an establishment, customs, and culture. Such engagement is limited by operative thinking (Meltzer 1986; Marty 1990) which sees individuality founder. Experience of life under these conditions would fluctuate on the basis of the prevailing basic assumptions and would also be expressed in bodily responses of adaptation, dysfunction, and lethal somatosis. Bion leads us to conceive of the personality as having further dimensions, with differentiations that aren't fully explained by the well-known distinction between the neurotic and the psychotic parts of the personality. We could contrast these as *groupality and subjectality* or, if one prefers, as a tribal sector and an individual sector. The construction of this model is exemplified in the conduct of borderline narcissistic personalities who dramatize in their external actions the disjunction of their psychic reality. It is also seen in the stereotyped forms of normopathy (McDougall 1989) which were observed and described some time ago in patients labelled "psychosomatic", as well as in the autistic features that coexist with apparently neurotic behaviour and symptoms. Such thinking disorders, with their elemental nature and ersatz character, are characterized by mimetic learning and seem to serve a primary defence, protecting the individual who becomes lost and is recovered as a subject in the continuous experience of himself and of others.

Hence, this *groupality* and *subjectality* would be present in every individual, and the nature of the personality as a whole would depend on the particular linking between each of these; whether this is a harmonious conjunction, a confusion or extreme disjunction between these two modes of psychic functioning. In the former case, groupality would have a constructive effect on individuality. But when groupality and subjectality become confused or are dissociated, the individual can't take himself as the subject of his internal group, and he behaves like a Pirandello-style author who can't give sequence or coherence to the characters of his inner drama. Quite to the contrary, he experiences the nerve-wracking pressure of his own groupality and, unable to metabolize or give meaning to this overwhelming anxiety and mental pain, he tends towards relations of complicity with other individuals in his internal group. Or, he will take refuge in the possibilities of the external social group (sports events, urban gangs, sects of whatever ideology) which have their own internal codes. This will exempt him from the harsh demands of working on his own individuality. The external group will take charge of his most primitive anxieties, redirecting these towards social ends. For example, the very existence of rival groups can justify the subject's anxiety and destructiveness, and identification with the idealized aspects of group culture are similarly protective.

Understanding of the personality as a whole must take into account the coexistence of the groupal and subjective sectors. This requires thinking about representative and phantasy life, on the one hand, and the external object, on the other, from the two vertices of individuality and groupality.

Bearing in mind both vertices must allow a binocular vision of the relational yields of psychic functioning and of its disturbances.

Yet, how can one achieve conjugation of the tribal vertex and the individual vertex which must secure the desired binocular vision? The linking of each vertex with the other must be accomplished through the establishment of relations, isomorphisms, and analogies between the two. Seen from this perspective, the achievement of binocular vision means creating a symbolic relationship between one vertex and the other. Such a relationship is in some sense a transferential, metaphorical relationship that brings closer and coordinates elements from the two systems, group and subjective, which had been isolated before the symbolic construction.

When the group analyst interprets the set of movements appearing in the session in a viewpoint that he singularizes with the name of *group*, he in fact takes on a role or assumes a function that may unfold in any relatively integrated person. In other words, it is not a question of whether, with our understanding of the group, we always make this connection between the mind of the individual and a supposed group mind. What I mean to say is that psychic functioning has some forms of production that are comparable with groupality, and others with individuality.

The link between one and the other functional sector or model of the mind has been explained sometimes as a container–contained relationship between very primitive parts of the mind which, in any case, have access to verbal expression, as if the more evolved part of the individual had the skills to capture the more primitive elements and formalize them. E. Jaques (1970) believes that herein lies the difference between the neurotic and the psychotic. The neurotic is able to manage and give expression in realistic terms to the psychotic part of his personality. In more recent literature, it is also postulated that prototypical forms of psychic reality would find form and expression in dreams, the contents of which relate to a preverbal mental area and which require symbolization of the preverbal or protomental (Bion Talamo 1992).

Groupality and *subjectality* should not be considered as being antithetical to each other; nor should movement between them be seen to indicate progressive or regressive movements. I think, rather, that they could be understood as forming part of a sequential rhythm of the mind in the style of a PS↔D oscillation. The individual is often unaware of this traffic in the mind which begins with a succession of scenes, or figurative representations of others and things. These representations are animated by the moment to moment state of the sensorial-perceptive flow, which in its turn determines the selection and quality of the image perceived. In this early stage of sequencing, the individual is subject to his own dramatized contents; is immersed and scattered between the characters of his internal world. But, in a second stage of the sequence, he comes out of this immersion, takes a distance, and is constituted as a subject who explains to himself and proclaims, like the coryphaeus of his own drama, what is occurring inside of him and what position he takes. The style of groupality is the dramatic flow of successive and simultaneous oneiric scenes which, forged in the unconscious, enter the realms of secondary process in a recitative or a more or less convulsive asseveration. This recovery of the subject as formulator of his own drama seems to correspond to the second PS↔D movement. Here, the characters of the internal drama are more greatly coordinated, thanks to one or several selected facts that give coherence to their interactions. This means that the individual is once again at one as a subject. His dramatized thought is exuberant, expansive and labile in its accumulation of images, but the moulded narrative of his discourse confers an orderly and more concise sequence to the formless quality of scenes in which the various contents of the mind interact. The depressive recovery of individuality is the systolic counterpoint to the at times more dispersive, proliferating paranoid schizoid movements of groupality.

This oscillation in the nature of experience from immersion in the scenes of fantasy to the recovery of the subject, also affects the style of interpretation that may be formulated in individual therapy and in group therapy. The interpretation given to the patient often interrupts his or her narrative and highlights a drama which is played out between patient and analyst in the real conditions of the session. In group therapy we more frequently see the transposition of a dramatic style of communication of the individual members, which is pulled together into a discourse by the therapist.

We see the group as a mind lacking a subject to narrate it and its development; and the group as actors or characters without an ego-author of the narrative that links them in coherent temporal succession. This subject ego has a twofold relationship with the mind. On the one hand, it processes and transforms the internal experience from an iconic language of concrete representations into a descriptive representation that gives sense to the drama. On the other hand, the subject can't live perpetually in his or her discourse and needs characters in order to signify the range of sentiments and affects he experiences. The subject is an author in search of characters. The level and nature of his anxiety will determine whether the movement towards others is collusive or, on the contrary, cooperative and to the benefit of the working group. I see the *groupality–subjectivity* binomial as a synergy that is close to, although not coinciding with the PS↔D oscillation but which, like the latter, consists in a necessary and desirable movement between positions which foster a beneficial dynamic for development.

In the group therapy setting, it is evident that when the therapist can take on the narrative function that describes the group drama, he organizes and condenses the multiplicity of interactions that have been produced in the group, making it a collective subject that he addresses in his interpretation. In fact, in the classic individual setting, the analyst describes and reconstructs the group dynamic in the mind of the analysand, which has been veiled by splitting and denial. This reconstruction involves the binocular vision that must be obtained by joining the two vertices from which the analyst considers the situation with the analysand. The example of E. O'Shaughnessy (1983) joining her view of the patient from H to K is an exemplary case of this binocular vision.

Another example is the link I have tried to establish between the vertex of groupality and that of subjectality with the stylistic variants of drama and narrative. Outside of the transference, in the family or social group, a good part of acting out can be understood as a collapse of subjectality, where the individual's internal group seeks refuge in collusion with the external group in a process that helps to drain away internal tensions.

Among Bion's great contributions to psychoanalysis, I have wished to draw attention to the concept of binocular vision achieved through the integration of vertices. Bion has singled out an essential condition for attaining such vision, namely the practice of maintaining free floating attention, understood as the unlimited freedom of thought that allows us to navigate among split-off parts of the mind, in "innumerable unfetterings", as the poet Carles Riba would say. Hence it is necessary to embrace this difficult maxim of being "without memory or desire". This recognition of Bion and the gratitude we wish to express to him in this meeting convened in his honour, derives not only from the highly suggestive contributions of his concepts and models. It also stems from his remarkable sincerity when expressing his difficulties as a working analyst in following his own technical axioms. Finally, we are grateful for his encouragement to walk through uncertainty before being able to construct the symbol in the session, and also to construct a body of theory that will make psychoanalysis a more and more independent science.

Note

1 Unpublished, October 1997.

Bibliography

Bion, W. R. (1952) Group dynamics: A re-view. *International Journal of Psychoanalysis*, vol. 33, 235–247.

Bion, W. R. (1957) Differentiation of the psychotic from the non-psychotic personalities. *International Journal of Psychoanalysis*, vol. 38, 266–275.

Bion Talamo, P. (1992) The creation of mental models: Basic and ephemeral models. Re-published in Bion Talamo, P. et al., *Maps for Psychoanalytic Explorations*, Routledge, London (2019).

Jaques, E. (1970) *Lavoro, creatività e giustizia sociale*, Boringhieri, Torino (1978).

Klein, M. (1958) On the development of mental functioning. *International Journal of Psychoanalysis*, vol. 39, 84–90.

Meltzer, D. (1986) *Studies in Extended Metapsychology: Clinical Applications of Bion's Ideas*, Clunie Press, London.

Marty, P. (1990) *La psicosomática del adulto*, Amorrortu Editores, Buenos Aires (1992).

McDougall, J. (1989) *Theaters of the Body: A Psychoanalytic Approach to Psychosomatic Illness*. W. W. Norton, New York.

O'Shaughnessy, E. (1983) Words and working through. *International Journal of Psychoanalysis*, vol. 64, no. 3, 281–289.

8 Notes on the Pathology of the Negative and Its Technical Approach to It[1]

Pere Folch Mateu

1 Introduction

In psychoanalysis the notion of the negative is characterized by intense ambiguity. If, on the one hand, it serves the mechanisms of various psychopathological disorders, on the other, we recognize virtue in mental functions and attitudes that are characterized by absence, or which are suspended. If negation, denial, and foreclosure are at the basis of the psychotic or perverse organization, we also value, in accordance with Bion, *negative capability*, considering that insight may be obtained through freeing ourselves of memory, desire, and the urgent need to understand. In this regard, negativity can be in the service of creativity, increasing our capacity for attention and presence.

It is not unusual to find expressions and concepts that express the paradox of the positivity of the negative, and the coexistence of creative and destructive aspects in negation. Negativity is one of the elements that constitutes any reality. One way or another, the negative marks its imprint, be it non-existent, latent or pejorative.

Even before his *Project for a Scientific Psychology* (1895), and indeed throughout all of his work, Freud never lost interest in the structuring value of an experience of loss; or in the mourning that is the basis of the installation of the internal object (*Mourning and Melancholia*, 1917). For Klein (1940, 1945), recognition of the loss of the breast coincides with the notion of the total object. The psychic life presented to us by Bion, so easily impregnated with negativity, illuminates investigation into syndromes like the Oedipal illusion (Britton 1989) and the invisible Oedipus complex (O'Shaughnessy 1989). Recall, too, the original contributions of Pierre Marty (1980) on essential depression, and also of André Green (1973, 1983, 1993), a great scholar of the negative, in particular his study of negative hallucination and his clinical approach to white psychosis, the dead mother complex, and so on.

Like light and shadow, positivity and negativity are embedded in the flow of our experience. As Lacan (1966) said, the word is a presence made of absence. This mutual involvement of absence and presence are part of

DOI: 10.4324/9781003342472-8

the dialectic of opposites that psychoanalysis has constantly highlighted. Of course, this is not only its most original contribution if we bear in mind that, from the Greeks to Hegel and through to the present day, philosophical thought has profusely pondered the negative. Hegel, cited by the Catalan philosopher Josep Ferrater Mora, went so far as to say that in every reality there exists a negation without which it would not be real: *the opposite in a reality is "internal" to it or, in other words, it constitutes it.* I stress this fact because of the everyday importance this maxim has for psychoanalytic thought. Practice confirms, as Robert Caper (2000) says, that we know things through their negation because, for example, without resistance we would not know the unconscious so well.

The presence of desire starts out from recognition of a lack while, in turn, desire channels and sectorizes our inner experience and makes us dismiss so many other possibilities for mental activity and the discovery of reality. For Unamuno also, negativity characterizes us: "we are a vacuum; we are what we lack". He thereby calls attention to the transcendence of the negative in our prospective orientation.

2 Clinical Aspects of the Negative

In clinical practice we find this entanglement of creativity and the pathology of the negative to which I have referred. For example, the experience of loss and desolation and the void, is the starting point for a re-creation by way of introjection of what is lost, ill-treated, or neglected. The eagerness for reparation that co-exists with any well-tolerated depressive anxiety thrusts us from an experience of the void into reconstruction of the link. Only when the primordial factor is deconstruction, dismantling and detachment from internal and external reality, are we fully immersed in pathology.

The original contributions of Bion (1962, 1963, 1967) have shown us, with the example supplied by psychotic patients, this deep embeddedness of the positive and negative of the basic drives: love, hate, and knowledge. Each may be known through its absence, just as knowledge may be stripped of sense. The clinical aspect, the perceptible expression of this denuding, is polymorphous, but may be expressed through withdrawal, in the cloistered life of the patient (Meltzer 1992), in the maintenance of a psychic retreat (Steiner 1993), and through insipidness, experiences of loss, a well-tolerated emptiness leading to psychic deterioration, an enduring somnolence, and a vague, somewhat sad coldness. Green has given order to this phenomenological repertoire of negativity, which he believes is expressed in the affective domain by indifference; at the level of thought, by white psychosis (which is characterized by the absence of delusion and anxiety, and aspires to the nirvanic); and in the realm of representation, as a negative hallucination aimed against the perception of inside and outside.

This kind of clinical picture is rarely presented as pure, with an absolute negativity. However, the ongoing void has led to perpetuated insipidness, or to states of mind in which suffering is denied by means of the mean-inglessness of the experience. But even in the most severe situations, there emerges from the very marasmus of negation a frail propensity to create a nexus. Turning to Freud's very early essays, Green believes that negative hallucination, conceived as the representation of lack, is consubstantial and necessary in bringing to life positive hallucinatory contents. And Bion (1970), by whom Green is sometimes inspired, from another standpoint, says that the absence, or negativization of memory, desire, and an eager-ness to understand, could lead one into a state of hallucinosis through which one could assume an empathic concordance with a psychotic state of mind. We could also add that in his *On Narcissism: An Introduction* (1914) Freud anticipated the scrambled confluence of positivity and nega-tivity, when speaking of the attempt to recover a connection with the lost object that may be contained within a delusion.

Consideration of the various proportions of positive (delusions, cata-strophic anxiety, guilt, et cetera) or negative symptomology (indifference, stupor, insipidness, meaninglessness, emptiness, et cetera) has led to clin-ical descriptions that come under the headings of positive or negative narcissism, life narcissism–death narcissism and de-objectification (Green 1983), and libidinal narcissism-destructive narcissism (Rosenfeld 1987).

The clinical picture is always mixed, and I shall return to this question when speaking of the technical approach to working with severe, border-line, or psychotic narcissistic pathology. But, at this point, I would like to propose that the therapist can consciously or unconsciously tend to head in one of the two following directions:

1   cooperating with the work of the negative, urging the patient to accept the manifestations of her negativity, or that which is exhibited as a deficit, as emptiness, as routine adaptation, tics of social coex-istence, and so on;

or, alternatively,

2   giving sense to what is positive in the delusion, and something more arduous, which is giving sense to the negative by approaching the subject's identification with an internal, subjugating aggressor who has been incorporated into his earliest object relations, passively trau-matizing him in childhood by absence or through the suspension of parental functions. The patient internalizes this aggressor and now feels that he is the victim of cruel absurdity and meaninglessness.

3 Induction to the Negative

In our clinical descriptions, if we are not very careful, we revert to the medical model, which is to say we consider the patient's symptom, her suffering, dreams, and conduct as detached from their context, from the world of their relations, and from the relationship with the therapist. Intellectually and with some conviction, we have gone beyond the idea of a unipersonal psychology and psychopathology but we lapse into a characterization of the patient and the clinical process in keeping with the old patterns of an observer (the therapist) and the observed (the patient). Even when we are thinking in the psychoanalytical or psychodynamic sense, we realize that, again and again, we are describing the patient; that we have emerged from a syntonic stance that is empathic towards her. In other words, we find it hard to accept that what the patient has been in the initial consultation or in a certain session, is the depiction of what has occurred between her and us; that schizophrenia, depression or the hysteria of anxiety is there between the two of us; that the meeting of our respective subjectivities has generated a link that we call phobic, delusional, indifferent, senseless, in a state of torpor, and so on.

It will be rightly said that the growing use of the countertransference has greatly modified the temptation to objectify the patient to some or other degree. But we relapse when there emerges in us different manifestations of unease, difficulties in tolerating the patients' requirements, the peremptoriness of their demands and their bitter disappointment in what we offer them. Unease also arises where we struggle to tolerate their amorous feelings, their aspirations of dependence, their tender docility, their craving to submit, and even their passion to know us and their longing for intimacy with us. In short, and perhaps especially, we avoid the difficult situation of these patients who are dramatically clinging to indifference, to a hopeless cohabitation, to an indefinite coexistence without desire, which unwittingly invites us into a certain euthanasia of mental life. These are the patients whom we later describe with various nuances under headings like white psychosis, destructive narcissism, and so on. When, as therapists, we flee the challenge these patients pose for us, flee from indifference to deluded logic, we respond, in fact, with a psychopathology of the negative or, in other words, we denude of sense that which could affect us with its mystery or could wound our own self-esteem.

The problem being discussed here, once we have shed this model of observation inspired by classical naturalist scientism, is whether we are capable, in our clinical work, of capturing the construction that has been made between the patient and ourselves in our meeting; of understanding the possibilities and limitations that have arisen where we have been invited to play a leading role.

My purpose is not to caricature the position of the solid organicist psychiatrist who, when a predominantly psychotic, characteropathic, or neurotic patient appears, basically tries to tell him *what he has*; what he is harbouring inside him, in his central nervous system, like a person who has a tumour or some kind of dysfunction. This notion that the patient "has something" and needs help to extirpate it or to accept it and bear it, presupposes a focus that can lead to a highly pragmatic position, but that is not to deny the humanity with which the patient's misfortune may also be compassionately understood. However, this theoretical focus may make the therapist insensitive to the demands of the patient who, explicitly or implicitly, comes offering a relationship of more or fewer dimensions, of greater or fewer expectations, uncertain in its destiny, but which can only be specified in accordance with the therapist's receptive availability. And, as I understand it, this is the case for all kinds of patients, including those who, at first sight, present themselves with the symptomatic façade of the pathology of the negative.

Our way of being affected by the patient's presentation moves us to accept it, reject it, or simply deny it. The psychiatrist may not realize that the delusional patient is offering a certainly difficult and perhaps stormy relationship. If we disregard this supreme or extreme demand for bonding, instead of taking on the challenge to make a delusional connection, we decide that the patient *has* a delusion, and proceed to its extirpation or suffocation by means of our pharmacological arsenal. If the medication is effective, what we in fact achieve is *whitewashing the delusion* and turning a tumultuous paranoid relationship into an insipid relationship of indifference and withdrawal. What was a delusional narcissism becomes a nirvana-like narcissism and a progressive diminishment of the relationship. Sometimes the evolution is not so straightforward and there are ups and downs that may motivate the therapist to seek doses and medications that establish with more or less precision a bland chronicity. This depends on many factors: maintenance of the sane, unharmed parts of the psychotic subject, her tolerance or intolerance of the feeling of emptiness that is brought on with the action of the antipsychotic cocktail, the therapist's capacity for hope, and his sensibility to the offers of relationship offered by the patient against all scepticism.

Clinical material

This is the case of a patient I have studied at length together with Joan M. Blanqué. He is a young schizophrenic man of 28, whose first attack occurred five years previously. It began with a very evident self-referencing delusion in which he attributed special significance and intentionality to fortuitous circumstances: the cinemas screened the films early so that he could not see the whole film, buses did not come, and the wait became interminable. God, "the Entity", wanted to harm him. It was probably because of the sins he had committed when he looked at some child pornography pages online. The patient also says that he has a split personality. God wanted to put him in a lunatic asylum; God had a very clear voice that spoke several languages.

In order to remedy this state of affairs, the patient received an antipsychotic depot injection every month and, according to him, this "violence I was obliged to suffer" induced in him an uncontrollable motor agitation. It was true that he no longer heard voices, as if "the Entity" had stopped its reproaches, but he felt exhausted by the agitation that had him constantly moving. In fact, he did not stop moving at all throughout the interview I shall describe. At the time of this interview, the voices have notably faded away and the patient is oscillating between a fidgetiness that won't let him rest and sinking into overwhelming fatigue that keeps him secluded in bed and far removed from any kind of initiative.

This is a typical case presentation of a delusionary relationship which has not been attended to but, on the contrary, has been annulled by medication. This is felt by the patient as the absence of an object, an object that now occupies the whole of his sensorimotor space in the form of this uncontrollable motility and the resulting paralysing fatigue.

This is what the patient communicates at his first meeting with the psychotherapist. He says that God does not talk to him anymore. "The Entity" must have gone quiet. "It doesn't say anything to me, but maybe it's nearby, waiting." In contrast with other patients who, with an anti-psychotic cocktail, lapse into a state of apathy and indifference, this patient has not been able to accept the new situation. The medication has not been able to do what it has done in so many other cases, namely to swap the delusional activity for routine automatism and increasing pas-sivity. It has stopped his delusional activity and, above all, has sus-pended mental activity in favour of a form of motor frenzy alternating with fatigue and sleep. To some extent this is a relief for his relatives, but when the patient feels accompanied by a therapist who does not pre-scribe medication, the memory of the ostentatious experience of delusion emerges.

When the therapist suggests that, despite everything, with the medica-tion he no longer hears the voices of God or the Entity that were threa-tening him, the patient says he has been suffering from chronic exhaustion for years: "It was precisely when the Entity came that my physical state improved, despite the worry about hearing its voice. But, since I've been taking the medication, I'm overwhelmed by exhaustion again. I think that this thing I have is a question of parapsychology. A parapsychologist I consulted told me that this thing of mine is a paranormal phenomenon, but you believe I'm schizophrenic and that I'm inventing the stuff about the Entity."

Faced with this difficult situation, the therapist decides to tell him that, as far as he understands, it is not just the Entity that is making him suffer but also the exhaustion that has so limited his life, leaving him isolated; it seems that he suffers a lot when he feels so alone.

This discussion began a therapeutic relationship with a wide range of possibilities where the symptom started to be linked with the patient's biographical vicissitudes and his particular way of trying to assimilate them. The depot medication was stopped, to the patient's great relief. The fatigue lessened but the hallucinosis did not recur. When the therapist asked the patient about the Entity, he said that he did not hear voices but that the Entity was appearing in dreams, which he was still unable to recall.

This is a particularly expressive example of an occurrence that is repeatedly confirmed when the prescription of antipsychotic medication is experienced by the patient as abandonment by the psychiatrist, and thus as an alienating treatment. Verification of this dates back for some years. As early as 1964, Diatkine and Paumelle warned that antipsychotic medication, when it is the only treatment, jeopardizes the patient's personal relationships and the possibilities of psychotherapy. They also pointed out that a delusion can safeguard psychic balance and that suppressing it can lead to stuporous depression.

As fragile consolation, we are told, year after year, that new antipsychotic drugs are free of side effects that cause psychic deterioration but, in general, clinical practice does not confirm this. Hence, systematic programmes of psychological support for schizophrenics have generously been introduced in Scandinavia following Finland's plan for the treatment of schizophrenia; and in different psychiatric centres in London, antipsychotic medication is reduced to an optimal minimum and support in the form of family therapy, individual psychotherapy, and sociotherapy is provided, depending on the particularities of the case and the nature of the psychotic process.

When therapists' insecurity, fear or anxiety obstructs contact with the explicit or implicit demands of the psychotic patient, there is a fleeing from contact. The therapist may take shelter in the idea that the evolution of the illness is unavoidable, and may try to treat or think he is treating the patient according to biological reductionism, as if biology were responsible for his psychotic suffering.

Let us not think, however, that this conscious or unconscious rejection of the patient's request for a relationship only happens as a result of the way the psychiatrist treats the psychotic patient. I believe that something analogous happens when working with those patients with less severe problems that are expressed within the usual parameters of the neurotic symptom, from situations of mourning to character disorders. Here, too, biological reductionism and the inability of public healthcare to offer attention as a form of treatment, can lead clinicians to ignore the patient's request; they then do not offer a connection that could lead to change. Once again, the patient's demand goes unheard and his message is answered with a chemical response in the form of tranquilizers and antidepressants.

Patients with less severe pathologies also feel the absence of someone who can listen to them. Without this, they can only introject the therapist's emotional deafness. Such patients become indifferent to their own psychic reality, and instead of inscribing their problems and conflicts in their minds, they live them out in their bodies, in their conduct, and in an attitude adapted to bear a neurovegetative system controlled by medication.

They then live with the senselessness of a disorder called anxiety, dystonia, stress or depression.

As I said before, this is not about caricaturing the role of the psychiatrist but about seeing this situation as paradigmatic of what can happen more subtly in the psychotherapeutic or psychoanalytic setting when, for some reason or other, we lose contact with the patient, with her indisposition; when we fail to respond to the invitation she offers us from the limitations of her discourse and general attitude; when our unease disrupts our capacity for emotional resonance and for being present to the conflict that the patient would have wanted to enact by assigning to the therapist in the transference a specific role through which to represent her inner drama. This patient, who does not know how to get her message through to us beyond the defensive possibilities available to her; who fails to awaken a vibrant reception in us which may transform her inner experience, feels abandoned once again to her desolate inner world.

I think that empathic support has often been misunderstood as a merely specular response. It is true that this conscious reception of the patient's situation and suffering, which moves us to be present and to accompany him in feeling, is unavoidable in any clinical act. But this entails making contact only with the patient's manifest expression and communication, providing the consolation of our compassionate presence, and perhaps suggestions for scrutinizing more broadly the horizon of his possibilities.

Hence, although it is very valuable, this does not correspond with the more specific thing the patient hopes to find in us. In fact, we have conceived a space for meeting, a setting that goes beyond this humanitarian aid. Thanks to this, we prepare ourselves to refine our sensibility, not only in terms of conscious communication but also in terms of the unconscious message that comes to us by way of projective identification. This message is not captured by fine-tuned observation of the patient's verbal and paraverbal expression alone but also requires us to make contact with what emerges in ourselves in response to her; with the impact we note that it has on our mood, on our fantasy, on the free-flowing or blocked tendency to harmonize with some or other object of the patient's. In this way, we do not limit ourselves to sympathizing with her defensive solutions, but also with the mental state underlying the manifest expression and implied anxiety; with the mental pain of various hues, compulsions, and so on; experiences which, not being tolerated, are not able to be consciously communicated but which only become evident through the ineffable path of unconscious transmission. This is a message that comes to us as an irruption, as an occurrence, as an affect that colours and invades our mental space to a greater or lesser extent.

When the patient's overall situation is, for us, something more than a story, something that inspires more than a commitment to help or emotional compassion because of what is happening to the *other*; when it inspires, moreover, recognition of something that is also happening to us with him, and when for the sake of the setting we have episodically come to be part of the patient's challenge, fantasy, or delusion, our empathy is more dynamic, more pressing. It is only then that, perhaps with better resources than the patient, we break the balance or the unfortunate symptomatic consensus in which the patient takes refuge. Our elaboration of her experience transforms the situation that comes alive in the transference, and it is this transformation, fostered by the conscious and unconscious taking on of what the patient is projecting into us, that will culminate in an appropriately formulated interpretation.

At this point, I cannot give an extensive account by way of illustrative clinical material, but I can offer a brief vignette which I believe is epitomic. I refer to a borderline patient who, after many years in analysis and as it neared its end, continued to have acute feelings of rancour about frustrations he had suffered at more or less crucial stages of his life. He said that however well things went for him, the memory of certain disappointments was so humiliating that it would never allow him to live with even moderate satisfaction. One day, at the start of the session, he surprised me with his expansive mood, which was somewhere between indifferent and even-tempered. He remarked on difficulties he had had at work the previous day, which he had managed without the usual feeling of upheaval and disquiet. He added, apparently without irony or sarcasm, that in the midst of his annoyance, he had had the feeling that he had achieved such a degree of strength that nothing could humiliate him: neither accidents, nor errors, nor embarrassments that might crop up with his colleagues at work or in moments of recreation. I was surprised by his change of tone, which affected his gestures. He was now free of the usual irritated twitchiness and his verbal style that was so often choked by emotion. In the session I am describing, he made a show of serenity and seemed to feel triumphant with his proclaimed imperturbability. Now, he was able to smile at any injustice, even though in practice it was so much against his own interests that common sense might have viewed this as foolishness.

When I recovered from my surprise but was still distracted by the unexpected nature of his expression; sometimes convinced, sometimes ironic, I wondered what identification the patient was acting out with his new behaviour. The memory of the previous day's session cleared up my doubt. In fact, I could recall the atmosphere of placidity I had felt at many points in that session, which had brought about the dissatisfaction of my previously only having accompanied the patient in his perplexity, without managing to offer him new perspectives from which to clarify his troubling feelings. Recall of such a smooth session with good, free floating attention to the mental landscape the patient described was not complemented in my own inner state and the ways in which it was evolving. Instead, I had a growing sense that with his serene and stoic attitude, the patient was caricaturing me. In other words, he was identifying with someone he experienced as an aggressor, which is to say with this attentive, compassionate character who never managed to be moved because he was only affected by observation of the conscious, observable, polymorphous message the patient was conveying to him, while remaining not very sensitive to the latent message that was coming via projective identification. It is a message that must be grasped by a periodic 180-degree change of direction in attention which can re-inspire our imagination, our curiosity, hope, edginess, or our own kinaesthesia.

4 Technical Approach

For the sake of brevity, I shall sum up those aspects that I think are most important in terms of technical guidelines when this psychopathology of the negative is predominant. At the risk of being too schematic, I shall limit myself to outlining the most pressing problems and the most ideal guidelines which, in my view, they lead to:

Avoid, as far as possible, the use of medication since it encourages the defences pertaining to destructive narcissism.

The problems raised here are:

a   how to avoid indifference and reorganize hope;
b   how to bring the patient closer to her catastrophic fears and despair, which are so strongly denied;
c   how to dismantle scepticism and nirvanic aspirations without inviting the traumatic situation of impossible desire. Or, in other words, how to avoid the brusque step from nirvanic narcissism to exigent longing.

What is required, then, is:

a   tuning in emotionally to the despair that is hidden behind the patient's indifference, passivity, and emptiness;
b   understanding the patient's extreme recourse when she is faced with a situation of despair; with her need to identify with an object that has been traumatized by indolence, depression, breakdown, and negativity;
c   bearing the indifference of the narcissistic patient and tolerating this, by acknowledging the message that is contained within the patient's acting out, for example when she makes us feel like the object of her dislike, like someone who reflects the harsh insipidness of her internalized primary object, and the emptiness and senselessness of her own Self, which sometimes stands out and is sometimes confused with the object;
d   approaching in the transference the problem of the symbiotic relation with the object prior to the catastrophic rupture that set off the narcissistic, negative reaction;
e   avoiding the overuse of antipsychotic medication in view of the negative consequences that it may have.

Note

1 Unpublished notes, 2003.

Bibliography

Bion, W. R. (1962) *Learning from Experience*, Heinemann, London.
Bion, W. R. (1963) *Elements of Psychoanalysis*, Heinemann, London.
Bion, W. R. (1967) *Second Thoughts*, Heinemann, London.
Bion, W. R. (1970) *Attention and Interpretation*, Tavistock Publications, London.
Britton, R. (1989) The missing link: Parental sexuality in the Oedipus complex, in J. Steiner (ed.), *The Oedipus Complex Today: Clinical Implications*, Karnac, London.
Caper, R. (2000) *Immaterial Facts*, Routledge, London. Catalan version: *Els fets immaterials*, Monografies de Psicoanalisi i Psicoteràpia, Viena Edicions, Barcelona.
Diatkine, R. and Paumelle, P. (2002) Médications et psychothérapies individuelles, *Revue Francaise de Psychanalyse*, vol. 66, no. 2.
Donnet, J. L. and Green, A. (1973) *L'enfant de ça*, Les Éditions de Minuit, Paris.
Freud, S. (1895–1950) *Project for a Scientific Psychology. The Standard Edition of the Complete Psychological Works of Sigmund Freud* I, 281–391.
Freud, S. (1914) *On Narcissism: An Introduction. The Standard Edition of the Complete Psychological Works of Sigmund Freud* XIV, 67–102.
Freud, S. (1917) *Mourning and Melancholia. The Standard Edition of the Complete Psychological Works of Sigmund Freud* XIV, 237–258.
Green, A. (1973) *Le discours vivant*. Presses Universitaires de France, Paris.
Green, A. (1983) *Narcissisme de vie, narcissisme de mort*, Les Éditions de Minuit, Paris.
Green, A. (1993) *Le Travail du négatif*. Les Éditions de Minuit, Paris.
Klein, M. (1940) El duelo y sus relaciones con los estados maníaco-depresivos, in *Obras Completas*, Paidos.
Klein, M. (1945) *The Oedipus Complex in the Light of Early Anxieties*. The Writings of M. Klein, vol. I. The Hogarth Press, London, 1985.
Lacan, J. (1966) *Écrits*, Éditions du Seuil, Paris.
Marty, P. (1980) *L'ordre psycho-somatique*, Éditions Payot, Paris.
Meltzer, D. (1992) *The Claustrum: An Investigation of Claustrophobic Phenomena*, Clunie Press, London.
O'Shaughnessy, E. (1989) The invisible Oedipal complex, in J. Steiner (ed.), *The Oedipus Complex Today: Clinical Implications*, Karnac, London.
Rosenfeld, H. (1987) *Impasse and Interpretation*, Tavistock Publications, London.
Steiner, J. (1993) *Psychic Retreats: Pathological Organizations in Psychotic, Neurotic and Borderline Patients*, Routledge, London. Catalan version: *Replegaments Psíquics: Organitzacions Patològiques en Pacients Psicòtics, Neuròtics i Fronteres*, Monografies de Psicoanalisi i Psicoterapia, Viena Edicions, Barcelona.

9 Containment, Acting, and Counter-acting[1]

Pere Folch Mateu

1 Introduction

The theme of this year's *Revista Catalana de Psicoanàlisi* conference is of markedly Bionian inspiration. The three terms, containment, transformation, and emotional experience, evoke core concepts of Bion's work which help us to understand mental states and the interpersonal processes that promote the development of psychic functions. In clinical work, they have a preeminent role in the evolution of the patient–analyst relationship and hence in the therapeutic process. Originally borrowed from semi-erudite everyday language, these terms have acquired increasingly specific meanings. Their repeated use by Bion and a growing number of his followers has required their conceptual delimitation, so that they have progressively lost their purely descriptive character to become bearers of more precise meanings. This has advantages but also some drawbacks. If the success of their dissemination is due to the fact that they help us to understand what happens in the mind, and what happens between two communicating minds, they have also become rather reified, as if they were at the service of a particular way of conceiving mental states and their coming into being. Accordingly, when we see them used in other contexts we are unsettled by the echo of their precise meaning in the particular vocabulary of a certain author, in this case, Bion. Questions also arise concerning terms designating related concepts but coming from different traditions. This is the case with the English words "containing" and "holding", which pertain to two lines of thought of frequent intersection, but which have slightly different meanings. It must be said, however, that the Bionian lexicon and concepts are circulating more widely and have been adopted within the psychoanalytic community by schools and authors of different backgrounds, from American adherents of ego psychology, to non-Kleinian British groups, through to French circles that are more or less close to Lacanian thought.

2 Containment: Prior Condition or Process

Taken literally, the notion of containment has a certain negative connotation, namely that of preventing things from exceeding certain bounds,

DOI: 10.4324/9781003342472-9

from going beyond a limit, or from dispersing. "Things" may be concrete objects, or they may be mental facts. The things of the mind are emotions, intentionalities, desires, beliefs, and drives. Since we imagine the mind in spatial terms, the containment we study is that which enables experiences to be lived within the mind, without spilling out from it into corporality, into specific action, or into hallucinosis. If containment is not understood within the wider framework of Bion's thought however, one might imagine that it is the prior condition for transformation, for the processing of emotional experience or, in Bionian terms, for the transformation of beta elements into alpha elements, as Britton reminds us. I think that containment coincides more with a capacity for tolerating uncertainty and for waiting with a "negative capacity"; with abstaining from ridding oneself of painful sensations or invasive moods until the work of *rêverie* has begun to endow them with meaning and make them thinkable. Certainly, the idea that a beta element, a raw emotional impact, cannot remain in the mind and must be expelled from it leads to the idea that it *could* be contained and transformed, and vice versa. In any case, the process of transformation is not limited to the conversion of beta elements into alpha elements. In fact, this is merely a first step in the direction of more creative mental activity that may emerge from more incipient forms of thinking.

We also know that containment of the chain of emotional impacts that affect us, whether intrapsychic or interpersonal, is a process, the attainment of which requires ongoing work. At any moment, the continuing stream of mental elaboration of experience may be suspended or turned against the flow. The mind is never hermetically contained. It would be more appropriate to say that the mind is an open container that spills over or decants into action. There are difficulties, therefore, when citing failures to achieve the sort of containment that would be most beneficial for the therapeutic relationship. This is why our understanding of the rule of abstinence has changed over the years, since Freud discussed *Agieren*. Acting out, acting in, dramatization and the assignation and temporary acceptance of roles by the analyst are various denominations for the means the mind has for expressing itself and expanding beyond the limits of a neatly symbolic verbal communication. Between contained expression in the service of transformation and elaboration of emotional experience, and expression that goes beyond the realms of thought, there are many possibilities.

3 Containment and Expression

The term enactment has been added to the long list of concepts which the psychoanalyst uses to understand expressions of the inner world. The analyst tries to distinguish what each expression conveys, and to work out which more or less specific action the subject is requiring him, as the analyst, to perform. This would correspond with the conative side of language or other forms of expression; that is, with the desire to modify in one way or another, the mind of the receiver, with a meaningful word, an inarticulate cry, or by hurling oneself into a specific action.

The title of the Conference is luminous: It refers to forms of containment which can transform the blind alleys and dead ends of defensive organizations, and offer new paths to experience and ways of processing it. It speaks to the containment of mental contents which may spill beyond the mind's borders and outside the space for representation which the analyst so carefully arranges when he organizes the setting. But a capacity to contain fluctuates, sometimes from one moment to the next, so that containment of oneself or the other becomes, at times, a matter of control, retention, and constriction of possibilities of experiences and expression.

The analyst's capacity to contain the patient within the limits of the setting depends in good part on his feel for maintaining the setting without rigidity. The analyst tries to ensure that the space of representation does not become a persecutory claustrum, no longer a space of freedom. But the difficulties of accepting the containment of the setting also depend on occasional or permanent difficulties of intrapsychic containment at the various levels of the experience.

4 Intrapsychic Containment and Expressive Containment

Green (1993), who was so often inspired by Bion, drew attention to this chain of serialized containments. He noted that the soma, with its wide range of chaotic stimuli and discharges, would be contained by the drive; in its turn drive would be contained by affect, that is, by elemental emotions that would provide an incipient meaning; emotion may then be contained by feeling that renders the meaning of the affect more precise; the containment of feeling would be found in the unconscious phantasy – thing representation – whose container would be the word representation – preconscious and conscious – in progressive degrees of abstraction. Green indicates, as does Bion through the elements of his famous grid, that each stage in the chain contains the previous one. At any point, one particular container may become less efficient, and an earlier form once more takes over. Symbolic thinking may break down as affects become uncontainable. There may be a regression to somatization and, ultimately, to death (recall Pierre Marty's (1980) psychosomatic organization and disorganization). The transformative containment that analysts try to provide in analytic treatment cannot but experience these same vicissitudes. The setting and the analyst are experienced as changeable; variously as a refuge or as restrictive, and the analyst too can feel constrained by the setting, the rule of abstention, and the risky paths of free floating attention and temporary role assumption.

5 Container–Contained in the Literature

At the intrapsychic level, these uneasy aspects of the container–contained nexus are experienced between parts of the self and internal objects, some of which have a containing function. At times, containment is felt as protective, at others, oppressive. A good literary expression of this conflictive container–contained relationship may be found in the universally recognized debate between body and soul. Britton (1992 and 2003, p. 100) refers to this in his paper, "Keeping Things in Mind", using as an example "A Dialogue between the Soul and the Body" by the seventeenth-century English poet Andrew Marvell. In Marvell's poem, both parties complain about their reciprocal imprisonment. Their dialogue exemplifies the vicissitudes of the container–contained relationship. We know about this from our everyday experience too, as we experience the relationship between our mental self and our corporal self. Do we have a body, contain a body, or are we a body? Do we have a body or does a body have us?

Britton's example is given credence by the very universality of the theme. In their dialogue, body and soul constitute a model of intrapsychic relational conflict, and also demonstrate the intrapsychic creativity of internal objects. In our literature, long before Marvell, this is a recurring theme. Thirteenth- and fourteenth-century Spanish texts concerning the dialogue between the soul and the body also present a conflictive relationship in which body and soul reproach and accuse each other, complaining about their inevitable coexistence. The theme is also to be found in Catalan classics, such as those of Ausiàs March and Jordi de Sant Jordi, where lyrical fancy once again takes up the soul–body debate. There too, it is clear that exchanges and conflicts are between different parts of the mind. As in the clinical setting, internal objects are personified and the dialogue between eyes, heart, body, and understanding is staged. In an inspired and illustrative work, our distinguished medievalist Lola Badia (2003) presents variants of this dialogue between internal objects that fill the verses of Jordi de Sant Jordi and Ausiàs March.

This digression through literary texts helps us approach a more precise understanding of the internalization of interpersonal containment. The prototype of this is, of course, the new-born baby whose needs and anxieties are projected into an understanding container breast, which receives and to some extent transforms his anxieties. The infant who is well contained, over time develops his own psychological functions and processes, including a preliminary capacity to contain himself. Interactions between internal objects develop in this context. In literary representation, poets stage the inner drama, unravelling it and showing how internal objects are related. In analysis, we try to understand the interaction between internal objects. We have learned, for example, that internal objects under the sway of paranoid schizoid anxieties link up and separate in ways that are different to those objects which are under the sway of depressive anxieties.

We wonder too about whether the creativity of internal objects that was so emphasized by Meltzer and Harris (1976), is accomplished in the context of containment and the oscillation between paranoid schizoid and depressive conditions, PS↔D. The classical dialogues of soul and body help us to think about the reciprocity which links two internal objects, which alternate in their function, sometimes containing, sometimes being contained. This is along the lines of the alternating functions of receiver and emitter in the process of communication.

6 Container–Contained and PS–D

Bion (1963, chapters 9 and 18) wonders in different passages, from the standpoint of the diachrony of mental development, what comes first: the container–contained relationship – via projective identification – or the oscillation between the paranoid-schizoid and depressive positions. It seems that he did not decide and in some places he affirms that the two are inextricable. However, what seems to be more than implicit is that the creative, processing function of containment itself passes through paranoid schizoid and depressive phases. The processing of any emotional experience which searches for meaning and demands to be thought, is brought about by means of the mobilization of several functions: memory, attention, imagination, inquiry, action, and so on, functions that jointly operate as a containing internal object. In the best of cases, the work of this container is carried out with PS <-> D fluctuations, from dispersion to integration, from disseminated expansion of the course of thinking to conjunction, and to the coherence of that tying up of loose ends which Bion called the *selected fact*. But this transformation, this generation of meaning has no end. On the contrary, it opens up new horizons for experience and fosters inquisitiveness. Questioning highlights further unclarity, which in turn mobilizes new containing processes by other internal objects. At the other end of the spectrum, disturbance or blocking of this PS↔D oscillation would be at the basis of the psychotic development (see *Cogitations*, p. 185). What also seems plausible is that restrictions in respect of PS↔D oscillations would give rise to object relational forms with scant elaborative, creative or even collusive possibilities. J. Aguilar (1996) considered this eventuality as one consistent with false containers. A. Grimalt and M. Miró (2001) also refer to this when they ponder deviations from the active work entailed by containment.

What we see in clinical practice, from which we can infer and in fact construct these vicissitudes of psychic life, is a more or less wide fluctuation of the container–contained chain schematized by A. Green. In fact, the varieties of enactment that may occur reflect the particularities of internal situations; interactions between different parts of the personality that become figments of fantasy, expressed in dreams and in the scene of transference. Clinical research is increasingly being brought to bear on the different forms of enactment linked with a range of pathological organizations. This naturally takes into account the analyst's receptivity, proclivities, and distortions in his or her capacity to take in the patient's projections. It further considers the analyst's capacity to assume a role, which the patient may nudge him or her to take on, and the fluency or viscosity of his or her free-floating responsiveness, in the sense used by J. and A. M. Sandler (1998, chapter 3).

7 Technique

I shall end these notes with some considerations of a technical order, which pertain to the empathic attitude of interpretation. When listening is empathic, there is first an early phase of concordance with what the patient is saying and doing in the session, followed by a second phase of de-identification by means of the meandering path of *rêverie*. The outcome of this way of making contact with the patient leads to interpretation; an interpretation that will remain *sotto voce* or will find an optimal time to be spoken.

7.1 Empathy and sympathy

It seems to me that to *either* offer the patient empathy *or* to interpret, makes no sense when empathic listening includes both phases I have mentioned. Passive, sensitive, in-tune and affectionate listening is not, as I understand it, all that takes place in the empathic listening process. Such listening would instead be sympathetic to the patient's suffering and misfortune, but would not include the analyst really experiencing or being affected by the patient's problems or conflicts. When one listens sympathetically, it is possible to remain full of compassion and charity. Such listening requires some skill, and is certainly respectful, but it may also remain at the level of dispassionate contemplation. It requires being with the patient but not in the patient, nor having the patient in us.

Empathy, by contrast, entails more than docile availability for the analysand's ongoing reflexive reproductions, which Sandler (1993) compared with a continuous, primary identification with what we keep perceiving. Some would regard this as a spontaneous inclination to which one is moved by an "impulse of consensuality". Empathic listening is characterized by moving between identification and de-identification; by the transformation that operates within us, that begins with the echo of a message from the other. The resonance model is apt here, since it helps us to recognize the fact that, in a peculiar way, the reality of the other is contained within ourselves, vibrating differently and transformed in the soundbox of our mind. Feeling affected, one does not simply reproduce what one is told and shown. Instead, one generates a new version of an experience recounted by the patient, which expresses the intentionality of what was said, and which reveals the patient's wish for the analyst to assume a particular role in his drama. This new version in which the analyst participates, also requires of the analyst that he stand outside the dramatization; in the wings of the stage of fantasy and of the session. When studying the pressure on the analyst to enact, Bodner (1999, p. 17) emphasizes that though he cannot always remain at an optimal distance from the transference drama, by virtue of being part of it, the analyst should be able, periodically, to recover his position as a spectator of it.

7.2 The psychoanalytic con-versation

The process of transformation of the patient's message does not begin with an interpretation but with the patient's way of seeing and hearing the analyst. Naturally, that depends at the same time on the analyst's way of being present. Interpretation, from this standpoint, is a two-person matter. Here, Resnik's words take on their full value: interpretation is an *inter-prestación* (an exchange of benefits); an ongoing construction with contributions from patient and analyst. I believe that this is close to the idea of Widlöcher (2001) who, following Freud's *Papers on Technique*, considers the analytic situation as a kind of conversation. I would say it is so, in the original sense of the word "conversation" (from the Latin, *con-versare*). That is, as a place where one "turns about with" another. Such meaning is related to the French *verter* and the Catalan *vessar*, meaning to spill or pour. Following the Catalan philologist Joan Coromines and going beyond him – perhaps engaging in wild etymology – we might say that the word "converse" could suggest a *co-vessar*, a co-spilling, by patient and analyst, of the contents of mental space; a spilling into the container of the setting in this updating, ongoing actuation or enactment that is the transference. Interpreting would then be directed towards what is happening in this confluence of spilled out thoughts, which have been poured into the conversation of the setting. As Thomas says (1995, p. 244), paraphrasing Bion, "interpretation would be naming what is happening, from a different perspective".

This co-spilling coincides with the idea of thinking together, with Widlöcher's *copensée* (2001, pp. 71–78), and it approximates to everyday Kleinian or post-Kleinian practice. The analytic task consists in an ongoing transformation of messages between analyst and patient. In analysis, this expressing, spilling, or pouring out of two minds can be contained within the analytic frame, within the elastic limits of the setting's containment.

I say elastic limits because though in the beginning, patient and analyst agree that the patient is free to say whatever he likes, whilst the analyst will adopt a relatively abstinent position, points may be reached where such freedom or abstinence become intolerable. These are moments of change or rupture in the possibilities of representation. At such moments communication may cease to be verbal or symbolic and the patient, and

indeed the analyst, may act out or breach the "rules" and earlier consensus regarding the setting. This co-spilling into the container constructed by consensus may turn into a spilling not only inside, but also
outside of the session; into enactments and counter-enactments. When
these are too stormy, they can no longer be analysed, for they do not
permit any reflective distance-taking. The analyst cannot find a third
position that allows him to be a spectator of what is taking place. In such
cases, in order to achieve a re-expansion of mental space, of the field of
experience, a wrangle between both patient and analyst is necessary. The
analytical conversation and, within it, the staging or enactment of the
patient's psychic reality and its internalized objects, is operative. Much
psychic work is required of both patient and analyst. Going beyond the
bounds fixed by our defensive organizations is risky, even in the analytic
framework.

Nevertheless, if the analysis is not stretched to the limits that are afforded by freedom of expression; if there is no transgression of balance, or of
the mental homeostasis of patient and therapist; no contravention or vio-
lation of the limits of defensive systems, the analytical process will be
blocked and the therapeutic relationship will only serve to consolidate the
defensive edifice that both patient and analyst, with their own characters,
have been constructing. This is the case with defensive collusions that
become chronic, in which patient and therapist unwittingly agree to skirt
around those situations that induce anxiety.

Many of the objections to the interpretative technique which is so central in today's Kleinian-Bionian technique are not related to this procedure
of empathic transformation. Criticisms instead seem to reference a psychoanalytic procedure dating back to before the Second World War, when
perhaps the interpretive ideal of quite a lot of analysts was the hermeneutic translation of the patient's discourse. Freud warned us of this: of
the symbolic interpretation of dream elements without associations, for
example. Though adherents of different schools of psychoanalysis criticize
what they regard as an excess of interpretation which Kleinians tend to
make, some theorists outside of psychoanalysis think that in fact, what we
say to the patient are not interpretations at all, at least not in the strict
hermeneutic sense. None other than Wittgenstein (1942) for example,
believed that rather than interpretations, the interventions the analyst
makes are rather clarifications, comparisons or approximations of experiences that are dispersed in the patient, which the analyst brings together
by establishing metaphorical bridges between different areas of the
patient's experience.

It seems to me that so long as the countertransference is not excessively
disturbing, today's Kleinian and post-Kleinian analysts avoid a hermeneutic translation of content and instead base their interpretations on the
rêverie that unfolds within the session. This means interpreting not only
the pre-conscious phantasies of the patient but also, and especially, the

way in which these phantasies are expressed in the interaction between analyst and analysand.

Certainly, interpretations that emerge in this way, out of the analyst's reverie, are very different from those which were common in the early days of psychoanalysis. Critics of a technique which is based on interpretation speak of the guilt-producing effect of interpretation. I think that when an interpretation does not spring from the joint experience of patient and analyst; from their ongoing con-versation, it is possible that guilt will be awakened in the patient. Certainly, where the patient is struggling to accept an interpretation, this may reflect a somewhat sadomasochistic balance between patient and analyst. More often, however, I would argue that an interpretation which is a hermeneutic translation promotes incredulity rather than guilt. The interpretations or clarifications that emerge in the analytic con-versation, both those expressed by the analyst and those which spill from the mind of the patient as a result of breaches of the boundaries of defensive organizations, may stir insecurity and anxiety. Empathic contact must serve to help the patient bear this disturbing newness, taking into account the patient's tolerance. If however, out of fear of bringing about an uncomfortable but promising situation, the analyst limits himself to sympathetically commenting on what he already knows about the patient, both parties may experience a sense of safety, but at the high price of impasse in the therapeutic process.

It is clear that in terms of the therapeutic process, we are today less concerned with questions of technique or with false dilemmas like empathy versus interpretation. What then are the therapeutic aspirations of psychoanalysis today? We know that they have varied over time and have been systematized (J. Sandler and A. U. Dreher, 1996) in the book titled *What Do Psychoanalysts Want?* What then are the aspirations of psychoanalysts and what are the aspirations of patients? It should not be forgotten that if psychoanalytic theory and technique have been partly the result of analysts' clinical research and theory for more than a century, clinical psychoanalysis is, as we see with interpretation, the fruit of joint work; a concern of both analysts and analysands. This joint work does not serve the same patients as it did in the first half-century of psychoanalytic practice. I believe that nowadays, mass access to public services and calls for the right to psychoanalytical help have somewhat changed the quality of the pressures on therapists and analysts during sessions, and this has repercussions in terms of the theoretical elaborations that these clinicians may make. The other pertinent question would then be: what are the aspirations of patients when these are inevitably conditioned by postmodern sociocultural patterns, and by the multifarious aspirations of human beings today? Such aspirations may be playful, hedonistic, epistemic, and so on, but they are also concerned with ethics, and may be coloured by cynical scepticism or tragic guilt about the third world.

The ego of today's psychoanalyst, like the ego Freud described in *The Ego and the Id* (1923) is subject to the command of three masters: (1) the aspirations and demands of present-day analysands, which express the sociocultural models in which they are immersed, and influence these analysands' ideas about what constitutes "cure"; (2) present approaches in science and philosophy which urge the analyst to reconcile them with his or her practice; and (3) the tradition of the psychoanalytical ideal, which is also being transformed over time. Psychoanalysis has to be practised first, with its patients and their ventures and misadventures in mind, and second, with the history and continuing elaboration of psychoanalytical thought itself in mind, as it faces the renewed challenges of clinical work.

Note

1 This paper was presented at the annual Catalan Review of Psychoanalysis Conference in 2003, which addressed the subject of Containment, Transformation and Emotional Experience. It was published in *Revista Catalana de Psicoanàlisi*, vol. XX, n. 1–2, 2003.

Bibliography

(This paper has relied in good part on documentation on the subject that has been furnished by studies by colleagues of the Barcelona Institute of who are particularly attuned to the problem under discussion. Although I do not mention them all in specific references, I have benefitted from this work while writing this paper.)

Aguilar, J. (1996) La funció de contenció, *Revista Catalana de Psicoanàlisi*, vol. XIII, n. 1.

Badia, L. (2003) De l'amor que educa a la passió culpable; Jordi de Sant Jordi, XI versus Ausiàs March IV, in *Memòria, escriptura, historia. Homenatge al prof. Joaquim Molas*, vol. 1. Universitat de Barcelona.

Bion, W. R. (1963) *Elements of Psycho-Analysis*, Heinemann, London.

Bion, W. R. (1992) *Cogitations*, Karnac Books, London.

Bodner, G. (1999) Imaginación y regresión en psicoanálisis, Lecture given to the Sociedad Española de Psicoanálisis.

Britton, R. (1992) Keeping things in mind, in Anderson, R. (ed.) *Clinical lectures on Klein and Bion*, Routledge, London.

Britton, R. (2003) *Sex, Death, and the Superego*, Karnac Books, London.

Caper, R. (1999) *A Mind of One's Own*, The New Library of Psychoanalysis, London.

Colin, James D. (1984) Bion's "containing" and Winnicott's "holding" in the context of the group matrix, *International Journal of Group Psychology*, vol. 34, n. 2.

Coromines, J. (1980) *Diccionari etimològic I complementari de la llengua catalana*, Curial ed., Barcelona.

Delattre, N. and Widlöcher, D. (2001) *La psychanalyse en dialogue*, Éditions Odile Jacob. Paris.

Freud, S. (1911–1915) *Papers on Technique. Standard Edition*, vol. XII.

Freud, S. (1923) *Das Ich und das Es. Gesammelte Werke*, vol. XIII, Imago Publishing Co.

Green, A. (1993) *Le travail du negatif*. Les Éditions de Minuit, Paris. In Spanish: *El trabajo de lo negativo*, Ed. Amorrortu.

Grimalt, A. and Miró M. T. (2001) Reflexions sobre el concepte de contenció i la seva aplicació a la Clínica. Lecture at the Institut de Psicoanàlisi, Barcelona.

Marty, P. (1980) *L'ordre psychosomatique*, Payot, Paris.

Meltzer, D. and Harris, M. (1976) The Educational Role of the Family, included in *Sincerity: Collected Papers of Donald Meltzer* (1994). Catalan version: *El paper educatiu de la família* (1989). Ed. Espax, Barcelona.

Resnik, S. (1978) La interpretación psicoanalítica, *Revista de Psicoanálisis*, Asociación Psicoanalítica Argentina, vol. 35, no. 3.

Sandler, J. (1993) On communication from patient to analyst, *International Journal of Psychoanalysis*, vol. 74, p. 6.

Sandler, J. and Dreher A. U. (1996) *What Do Psychoanalysts Want?* The New Library of Psychoanalysis, London.

Sandler, J. and Sandler, A. M. (1998) *Internal Objects Revisited*, Karnac Books, London.

Thomas, J. (1995) *Comentarios sobre "Elementos de Psicoanálisis"*, EEIPP, Madrid.

Widlöcher, D. (1996) *Les nouvelles cartes de la psychoanalyse*, Éditions Odile Jacob, Paris.

Winnicott, D. (1971–2001) Transitional objects and transitional phenomena, in *Playing and Reality*, Classic Books. In Spanish: Objetos transicionales y fenómenos transicionales, in *Realidad y juego*, Gedisa ed.

Wittgenstein, L. (1942) Conversaciones sobre Freud, in *Estética, psicoanálisis y religión*, Ed. Sudamericana.

10 The Lyrical and the Logical in the Work of Interpretation[1]

Pere Folch Mateu

Introduction

The aim of this paper is to highlight stylistic differences in the way analytical work is conducted. Such differences begin to appear from the moment the analyst starts listening and persist until the interpretation is formulated. In the countertransference, the analyst becomes aware of fluctuations in the way he receives the patient's communications and reflects upon these, and in the way he expresses himself. Such fluctuations are more or less moderated, but they may give rise to omissions, or inopportune interventions. I want to situate the way in which the analyst is affected by and responds to his patient between the polar opposites of the lyrical and the logical, depending on whether his responses are more or less characterized by creative, imaginative resonance, or are constrained by conceptual rigour.

I wish to link my notion of the lyrical and the logical to aspects of paranoid schizoid and depressive mental functioning, and of course to Bion's concept of oscillation between these two types of organization (PS↔D). The coexistence of the lyrical and the logical, and the conflicts and alternations between them, find a more or less precise echo in the opposition between unrestrained emotion and common sense. The vignettes included in this paper illustrate fluctuations between the lyrical and the logical, which influence and characterize variations in analytical style. Such fluctuations depend on the vicissitudes of the session and, in particular, on the analyst's variable capacity to resonate with his patient. A final, longer vignette illustrates movement along the lyrical–logical spectrum. It highlights congruences and conflicts between these opposites, and dramatizes one interpretation in order to demonstrate my meaning more clearly.

Interpretative Work

Interpretative work begins with the analyst's capacity to engage emotionally with his patient. Both this capacity, and the *way* the analyst is affected

DOI: 10.4324/9781003342472-10

by his patient, foster the emergence of an unconscious waking dream, in the Bionian sense (1965, 1992). This more or less corresponds to the state of reverie. This would be an initial stage of the work, which is followed by a second stage consisting of the communication of this waking dream to the patient. But this reverie, this dream, just like a nocturnal dream, undergoes a secondary review, which will serve to shape a third stage: the formal interpretation. Freud (1900) saw the secondary revision as a means of making the content of the dream comprehensible and sufficiently rational, in accordance with the requirements of secondary process. At the same time, he regarded this revision as aiding the interpretation of the dream, so as to assuage and render tolerable to the conscious mind the phantasy that is latent in the dream.

From the listening stage to the voicing of the interpretation, the mental activity of the analyst follows a trajectory that is comparable to that of anyone who dreams, whether asleep or awake. It is affected and impacted by the patient, and is elaborated in the language of unconscious phantasy. This unconscious phantasy charts a complex pathway towards presence, towards consciousness, towards that which the conscious mind can tolerate. If an interpretation derives from the analyst's waking dream, and has been worked on by his alpha function which has transformed the impact made upon him by the patient, how is the protean, evanescent emotional experience of the session visualized internally and then expressed in words?

The dream and the reverie of the analyst have some features in common with processes that are at work in the patient. It is true that our technique, and the technique that we would like our patients to learn, have many things in common; in fact, we think that the more free floating our attention is, or the closer it is to the state of grace which Bion (1967) believed was characterized by the absence of memory and desire, the freer the thought and associations of the patient become. However, although whatever the patient expresses in their words and silences is acceptable, and indeed welcome within the setting, the same is not true of the analyst, who must learn to remain silent and to speak only when it is opportune to do so. This is one of the many senses in which the interaction between the patient and the analyst is asymmetrical: the latter is responsible for using the knowledge he possesses in the service of the patient. There is a professionalism about his use of phantasying which distinguishes the way he conducts himself from the way the patient does. There is also a professionalism in his use of words which, in certain respects, is not unlike that of the poet, something which Freud drew attention to in 1907. Like the poet, the analyst works "with working hands on words" (Vinyoli 1973), and when things go well, he can say "I patiently sift through the debris and then I build again".

One of the relevant aspects to bear in mind with regard to the internal attitude and work of the analyst, is the gestation and development of the interpretative work, which culminates in an articulation to the patient.

This is an aspect to which Pere Bofill (1962) has been drawing our attention for many years, since our joint (1962) communication concerning countertransference. The present comments mainly concern what we could understand as matters of style: the receptive, cogitative, and expressive style of the analyst. They address how we engage emotionally with the patient; how we process in our reverie that which has affected us; and how we communicate or express the thoughts that our reverie has brought to mind.

The Lyrical and the Logical

In highlighting the lyrical and the logical, I am referring to two contrasting nuances in the analyst's receptive, cogitative, and expressive style. The poetic, or lyrical way of engaging would be, initially, expressed through the analyst's intimate emotional resonance with the patient. It may be characterized by a certain anarchy, whether calm or agitated; the analyst's attention is dispersed, indeed prefers heterogeneity. His resonance is rich in unsuspected reflections, which discover a secret affinity with those things revealed by symbols (in the words of J. N. Santaeulalia (1989)); it is a state of mind in which living an experience takes precedence over understanding it.

In contrast with this poetic manner of engaging, there is a tendency to organize and hierarchize; to impose descriptive or rational sequences on the diverse stimuli that affect us. The desire to understand predominates, and it constrains the expansive development of the lived experience. If lyrical and logical can be contrasted in this way, it should also be borne in mind that they need each other. Lyrical expansion scatters, and naturally cries out to be organized by a thought. Likewise, the poet who is carried away by, or visited by inspiration, and by messages received in phantasy, needs to give form and limits to his phantasying via the rigour of the word and the strictures of poetic discourse. Some poets, such as Carles Riba (1953), speak of a lyrical process which begins with a message drawn from the preconscious, which has been delivered to the conscious mind as a dreamlike offering. In order to become a poem, the offering must allow itself to be subjected to a conscious working over; to the painstaking vigilance of thought, whose linguistic resources can finally bring it to expression.

J. Freixas (1995) addresses this issue when, in reflecting upon the liminal position of the symbol between the inner and the outer world, and between dream and language, he raises questions about the violence that the symbol inflicts both on language and on the dreamlike state. Julia Kristeva (1974) broadens the horizons of these suggestions by showing us that this violence is bilateral. In fact, she argues, the symbol also suffers violence from the sensorial elements of experience. This leads Kristeva to reflect upon the dismantling and remodelling of the symbolic by the semiotizing impact of language. This matter is of great importance as the analyst reflects upon the style of the interpretative language he uses, though it is beyond the scope of this paper to elaborate further. The contributions of J. Coromines (1991) on auto-sensoriality and its impact on thought and word, also touch on the technical problem of how to verbalize an interpretation. What I am wondering is whether, in order to give vibrancy to the analyst's expressive capacity, the interpretation should include phonic, rhythmic and tonal elements which are consonant with the analyst's unconscious sensorial experience. An interesting clinical example of this is given by V. Hernandez (1992), who contrasts "sensorial" symbols with "metaphorical" symbols.

To speak of the lyrical and the logical is to highlight a stylistic contrast between logical processing as an ordering, syntactical and rational function on the one hand, and another way in which experience and word are actualized: a more effusive way in which syntactical ordering gives way to semantic disruption, to the unexpected, and to metaphorical leaps. At different stages of interpretative work, the lyrical and the logical poles vie with each other for predominance in the mind of the analyst. Logic strives to give shape to intuition in the form of discursive thought. If logic were to predominate, the analyst's interventions could be interrogating, even intrusive. They could be too influenced by rationalistic reductionism, intolerant of contradiction and paradox. By contrast, when the lyrical predominates, the unconscious permeates the phantasy-imbued inter-subjectivity of patient and analyst. The lyrical and the logical, in their interaction and correspondence, could be likened to the cyclical beating of the heart; to a paranoid-schizoid diastole and a depressive, organizing, retreating systole, around which a selected fact may crystallize. As I shall explain, this does not mean that I am equating logic with a depressive integration of the inner experience.

The logical and the lyrical could be loosely compared with the frequently recalled sense-versus-sensibility binary. They not only denote behavioural styles but also ways of being emotionally affected, that is, receptive styles. Sensibility would be closer to the language of poetry, sense to the world of logic. The coexistence of sense with sensibility, or logic with poetry, is complex. The poet J. V. Foix (1936) was particularly interested in this binary, and one of his poems alludes to it explicitly: "If only I could make reason and folly agree ..." Gabriel Janer Manila seems less anxious about this coexistence, and writes of, "the folly that one can put into poetic play". When it is driven by intuition, sensibility reminds me of what Bion wrote about the mad sane parts of the personality. Paul Valéry (1937) also approached this idea when, in the opening class of his course on Poetics at the Collège de France, he said of the soul that "disorder is the condition of its fecundity: it contains the promise of this fecundity, which depends more on the unexpected than on the expected, more on what we do not know than on what we know." Other poets have spoken of this to me in a different sense. I remember asking Palau i Fabre what he thought of lyrical reason, and he said that he felt it as incongruence.

When I refer now to logical style or to poetic style, I do not consider them to be mutually exclusive: it's really about the predominance of one over the other, but without ruling out the opposite style. Thus, both styles remain interwoven. When the influence of either the logical or the lyrical is overwhelming, we are dangerously close to psychopathology. Thus, an obsessive personality may exhibit a predominance of the logical, while when in a passionate state, in or certain depressive states or narcissistic structures, the lyrical attitude cannot easily be tempered by logical discourse. Liberman (1978) has nuanced this binary, finding no less than six communicative styles along the lyrical–logical continuum. These styles he associates with the great syndromic vectors of psychopathology. He also regards the coexistence of different styles as a regular phenomenon, and speaks of a latent style and a current or manifest style.

The coexistence of logical and lyrical styles can also involve conflict: the logical imposes strict constraints on the poetic, or the latter becomes a sort of mischievous child which needs logic to take care of him. At best, the logical and lyrical veins can coexist in a successive or reversible container–contained relationship, in a Russian-doll-like formation. As I previously noted, this coexistence, the alternating succession of the logical and the lyrical, would correspond to a good PS↔D synergy in the Bionian sense. Undoubtedly it would be appropriate if, during the interpretative work, there were a time for poetic predominance and a time for logical predominance; a time for lyrical expansion of inner experience, and a time for verbal communication. In fact, in verbalizing an interpretation, one must not only express simply and clearly what one wants to say in relation to one's waking dream; one must also adapt to the lexical and discursive ability of the patient. One must do this on occasion even where one senses the patient's reluctance to listen and understand. And it goes without saying that any inclination to embellishment on the part of the analyst is entirely inappropriate. As Ogden points out (1999), choosing exquisite language betrays the enacting of a narcissistic countertransference.

The point is that the poetic and the interpretative tasks of analysis are different. We might be affected poetically in the initial phase of the interpretative work, just as a poet is affected by external reality or by his own dreams, but in our case the purpose of the intervention is far removed from poetic form for its own sake. An analogy can be drawn between the way in which one is affected by reading a poem, and the way one might afterwards discuss the meaning of the poem. Similarly, whilst one is affected by the development of a session (see Ogden in the work referred to above), or by the creations of a patient (like the 7-year-old child I was treating who made a plasticine duck with four legs, bursting with movement, which symbolized the anguish-free mobility which the four sessions had achieved for him), the way we speak about the creation must be measured. Our attention should be focused on clarifying the situation that we are confronted with, and are sharing with the patient, clouded as this may be by their defence mechanisms and by our deficiencies.

At other times, the poetic language of the patient, the increased use of metaphor in his discourse, triggered by an anguish which draws everything in, including the analyst, may make the analyst less receptive than he would like to be. I offer the following example to illustrate this:

I was beginning a psychoanalytical treatment with one of my first patients. Even though a latent psychotic state had been ruled out, the patient experienced moments of overwhelming anxiety. During one session, he started to pose questions about his insecurity and the dark, vague premonitions which assailed him. One day he steeled himself and tried, without much conviction, to express what he was experiencing. After a silence, he told me, in a trembling voice, that he had the strange feeling of having been stretched over ten square kilometres. Presumably on account of my own anxiety at witnessing the emergence of psychotic anguish, I said to him: "Breathe deeply!" The patient did as I asked and his anguish quickly dissipated, but it was also clear that the opportunity to more fully understand the very concise, eloquent message that I was receiving from him had been lost. In the face of this lyrical condensation of his distress, I had become silent and mentally disengaged; lost in a bewildering sequence, unable to offer containment or understanding.

But the interpretative task of the analyst differs from the meticulous, often prolonged, activity of the poet, who may become lost in the process of sculpting words. The poet, though he may round off each stage in the process of poetic creation, may have an indefinite period of time in which to write. Analysts, by contrast, have to articulate their waking dreams in the fleeting moment of a session when communication is most appropriate, when it is most likely to be effective.

However, if the differences between poetic expression and the third stage of the verbal interpretation are great, the analogies and coincidences between them are evident in the first and second stages of analytic experience, which I tried to delimit within the interpretative process as a whole.

The first stage, especially if we aim to follow Bion's advice (1967) and attend without memory or desire, is a period characterized by ignorance, in which progressive or sudden elucidations are always so partial that they leave ample space for mystery. Here there might be certain aspects in common with the way the poet is affected. The poet is open to the dream, as Freud writes, and as the poets themselves have explained in greater depth. Yet if the poet, as Janés i Olivé states (1936), can "open [his] eyes wide to the dream", the analyst can only do so partially or intermittently, like the hare that sleeps with one eye open. To put it more precisely, he has to inhabit a complex simultaneity: He must be open to reverie *and* offer an observant, receptive presence in relation to what the patient says and does. The analyst must be present in these ways both when the patient's communications are clearer and during those foggy moments when the analyst and the patient are, to express it once again in the words of a poet, "the hosts of the same mystery" (Carles Riba, 1937).

I often recall a young girl whom I treated from the age of 9 into her early adolescence, to whom I referred more extensively elsewhere (Folch 1990). The girl often expressed herself lyrically, and in one session at the end of the week, had refuted an interpretation. I drew her attention to her defensive strategy when faced with the anguish of separation, alluding to the manic way in which she distanced herself from her objects and from me in the session, placing herself far away in what she herself called her dream, in which I was represented as a vague shadow. When I pointed this out to her she became agitated and almost shouted: "No, no, no, you are not a shadow, not at all, you are very real. The thing is that you are dreaming too ... yes, yes, we met, really and truly met, during our dream".

The second stage of the interpretative work affords us, in a rather more reflective or enquiring manner, a closer awareness of the meaning of our reverie. Bodner (2000) stresses the importance of imagination in the intentional search, by the analyst, for symbolic meaning in the unconscious phantasy of the patient. If I have understood him correctly, this would correspond to the second phase of the process I have been describing; one in which the most poetic and regressive aspects of the analyst's reverie interlock with the beginning of a logical orientation, reaching towards a reflection that has more to do with secondary process.

It should be said that the analyst, when he allows himself to become immersed in his own dreamlike meandering, is in a rather symmetrical situation to the patient. In the analyst's waking dream, which develops out of the remnants of the patient's reflections, he discovers correspondences with that which the patient is explaining or inferring. It would seem that both patient and analyst need to metabolize the direct, here-and-now relationship by connecting to situations that are remote in time and place, in order to more fully understand what is happening in the session. Ogden (1999), in the same paper I commented on earlier, offers a good clinical example of this procedure. Maybe the little girl I was treating was alluding to this, unwittingly but in a moment of inspiration, when she said tenderly that we had really met in a dream. Such moments are poetic, but they also call for more descriptive, rational reflection upon the scene that patient and analyst are enacting in the course of their interaction. I would suggest that it is at this point that the logical takes over. Then, cognition is distilled from an emotional experience. New horizons of experience can be glimpsed, and new uncertainties too. These will then also have to be addressed, perhaps lyrically. Of course, logic should not become a straight-jacket for poetic expression, nor should the poetic message be reduced through the application of theory.

We have been talking about styles, both lyrical and logical, but *which* logical style should the analyst ideally use? Or which styles? The Aristotelian, the Newtonian, the Russellian, the inductive, the logic of the unconscious? I recall the profound and systematic reflections on the problem of interpretation by Coderch (1995), whose book was a frequent companion while compiling these notes; and the inspired studies by Tizón (1978) and Jorge L. Ahumada (1999). These serve as excellent guides for anyone beginning to plumb the depths of psychoanalytical epistemology, and in particular, of the logic of interpretation and enquiry. I have recently devoted detailed attention to the work of Ahumada (Folch, 2001) and will only now point out his recommendation that the analyst identify variance in the logical quality of his receptive and expressive styles, and should in particular reflect upon the most viable ways to acquire an ostensive insight.

So far I have devoted little time to considering the third stage of the interpretative process, which begins with the interpretation as it takes shape in the mind of the analyst and ends with the formulated interpretation. Sometimes the analyst will prolong this stage. He may have a clear formulation in mind, but may not quite be able to arrive at an interpretation with which he is satisfied. Possible interpretations may not withstand his criticism, and may only be accepted once they have already been confirmed by further material from the patient. The analyst finds this delay difficult to deal with. He is constrained by the need to feel very sure that he is right before offering an interpretation to the patient. During this time, it is the logic of the analyst's cogitative style that predominates. At other times, on grasping the meaning of an internal situation that the patient dramatizes, the analyst might too quickly communicate the "truth" that he has grasped or constructed. These are moments of lyrical predominance, which lack logical moderation. When the lyrical and the logical do not interact appropriately in the mind of the analyst, the unconscious tension might lead the analyst to betray himself with a lapse, unhelpful to the patient.

By way of example I could cite not infrequent cases of colleagues who are beginning a psychoanalytical career, who say that they have never managed to interpret in the context of a particular session because they always wait for the patient to provide further material that might justify the interpretation they have begun to elaborate. They wait so long that the session ends without their finding an appropriate moment to intervene. At other times, the difficulty of harmonizing intuition, which arises unexpectedly, with a minimally logical language that might make it comprehensible, causes a *lapsus linguae* or a failed act. This has happened to me in fact. I once found myself saying to a patient that she had left her baby in a discotheque. The patient, as surprised as I was, politely corrected me and said that she had left her baby in a kindergarten. We may make shocking slips of the tongue especially when we are interpreting, and it is cold comfort to say that at least we are honest enough to reveal what we really mean. We must take advantage of such slips to work on the countertransferential motivations.

As well as the unconscious activity which determines, as I have pointed out before, the secondary revision of the analyst's waking dream, the analyst's conscious reception of insight is also important. The degree of conviction or doubt with which he experiences insight matters. The unformulated interpretation enters the mind of the analyst and is variously met with belief and the hope of gaining greater knowledge, or with scepticism and misgivings. If, as Britton (1998) says, an interpretation reflects the belief of the analyst, then the degree of conviction, ambivalence and uncertainty he feels about it will also be reflected in the rhythm, tone, and even the grammar of the formulation, and in the final interpretation.

If the correspondences that we can establish between our reverie (activated by projective identification from the patient) and our imagination seem largely credible to us, the time that passes between the discovery of a selected fact and the formulation of an interpretation will be short. The interpretation will be articulated in the present tense without too much caution. However, if our belief in the unconscious element we have discovered is less certain, we will tend to word it in a subjunctive or conditional tense. The delivery of the interpretation will also be affected by our degree of conviction. This will be heard, for example, in the more sensual aspects of interpretation such as emphasis, tone of voice and prosodic variation. A lack of clarity in what we have understood can cause us to adopt an excessively exhortative tone. By contrast, when what we want to say presents itself to us internally as a clear insight that might bring new knowledge to light, the verbalization of it does not need any rhetorical device to enhance its expressive force.

The analyst's communicative style may depend on the degree of verbal improvisation or intra-psychic prefiguring of the interpretation before it is articulated. Some analysts report that when they begin to interpret, they hardly know what they will end up saying. It is as if the words organize themselves during the act of speech itself. At a certain moment during the session, the analyst may simply find himself speaking.

Here we find a certain similarity with the activity of the poet. Frequently, the poet does not know what he wants to say until he actually says it. Carles Riba (1937) asks himself whether the word goes before or after the experience. He says that we do not believe until we have said what we believe. Thus, "I believed therefore I spoke", as opposed to "I spoke therefore I believed".[2] More recently, in the correspondence between Joan Vinyoli and Miquel Marti I Pol (1977), reported by Ferran Carbó (1990), we find the wonder of the poet on realizing that the "found" word tells him what he wanted to say. To put this in Freudian terms, only the representation of the word can make us conscious of the representation of the thing.

Returning to the clinical situation, when the analyst allows himself to be in a state of reverie and finds, in his waking dream, correspondences with that which the patient is explaining or implying, he finds himself in a symmetrical situation to that of the patient. As previously stated, in order to further understand what is happening in the session, both analyst and patient need to metaphorize their direct relationship in the here and now in situations that are displaced in space and time. When E. Torras (1992) highlights the creative value of the symbol and its ability to represent and connect the respective emotional experiences of patient and analyst, she is recognizing the significance of this creative cooperation. She is highlighting that this displacement of their most immediate and striking experiences during the session are not only defensive.

Clinical Case

I think it a happy coincidence when a good synergy between the logical and the lyrical in the thought and feeling of the analyst, makes it possible to link the patient's relational scenarios (external and internal) with their enactment during the session. When this happens, a formal interpretation may take on a dramatic style.

In order to illustrate this, I will describe in detail part of a supervised session in which receptive and expressive styles were interwoven harmoniously. In the session fragment that I report, the patient (a trainee psychotherapist) explained that his wife had attended a lecture given by his analyst. He said:

> She came back very excited, praising the way you developed the subject, and especially the fact that it was so humorous and enjoyable to listen to, so much so that you had the audience laughing several times. It's sad that I never met that analyst with such a great sense of humour. Instead, I ended up with a grumpy, surly analyst who saves his friendly, funny side for other occasions (Pause) My job isn't going well. I've just had a psychotherapy session with a patient who was curious about my private life. He told me that he had the impression I was from a modest family. He said that he had overheard that I had been born in a doorway in the Eixample. I recognise that if what the patient said was true, I would feel very uncomfortable.

The patient in this session (the trainee psychotherapist), made some comments about tense feelings and relaxed feelings in the treatment of patients. The tone of the conversation was starting to languish when he said, "Ah, I had a dream last night. I was walking along a street with my wife and for some reason she was walking a few steps ahead of me; perhaps I had lagged behind to look in a shop window. My wife was moving with difficulty ... in fact, a few days ago she sprained her foot and now she limps because of the pain ... but I told her that the way she was tiptoeing was like Mephistopheles with a goat's leg. (He laughed) I realize now that my jealousy betrayed me; I think that when she explained to me that she had been to your lecture I felt jealous and that was why I was making fun of her limping."

The analyst said nothing. He did not speak of the patient's jealousy; he had the feeling that the patient's conscious awareness of rivalry, and his depressing sense of being excluded from the analyst's private life, were making him reflect in ways that were less than obvious.

P: [He was taken aback by the silence] ... Is this analyst a canny old dog with the same seductive power as old Faustus, and if so, by what good or evil magic arts?

A: [Still saying nothing, he felt an uneasy curiosity, and then found himself asking,] But why did you refer to a goat's leg?

P: Well that's how the devil is always represented. Even when he comes to Dr. Faustus's house in disguise, you can see his goat's leg under his tunic.

A: [Emphatically] It's not a goat's leg. It's a horse's leg!

P: [After a silence] ... Yes, you're right, I have to admit it ... I still remember reading a bad translation of Goethe which spoke about Mephistopheles and his horse's leg ... (a brief silence) ... (with a mocking laugh) I must say that I am surprised by your question and your clarification about the devil's leg ... But then again maybe I shouldn't be surprised because it fits perfectly with what I know about you and your interest in horses and, of course, if I mistake one of your horses for a goat ...

A: [He continued not to speak about jealous rivalry, but to be convinced by his previous intuition] I think you are using the session to satisfy your curiosity about my inner life: about what I'm thinking now, my hobbies and preferences, a bit like your patient was doing. But you're not doing it openly, as he was, in asking questions about your past; you are doing it in a more subtle way, through your mistake about the devil's leg. In this way you have been dramatizing the insecurity that leads you to a voyeuristic control over your objects ... but you have very carefully disguised this...

P: [Pause] ... Now you have thrown me off balance ... what was clear to me was my unconscious jealousy and my rivalry ... but now I'm not sure what you are saying to me ... unless you are accusing me of, as you often do... how can I put it? ... accusing me of Mephistophelian insidiousness? ... Well, what can I say? I don't understand your interpretation.

A: [In an impatient, irritated tone] It's as if our dialogue had been like this: is your father a goat? No! He's a horse!

P: [He burst out laughing loudly.]

A: Now I'm the one who doesn't understand what you find so funny

P: It's because now I can see everything so clearly! ... And to be honest, I am grateful to you because you have been so fair today; in your lectures you may be funny, but just now you have given me as much, or more than you gave my wife. I don't know if I'll be able to resist the temptation to tell her ...

The session continued, dense and rich in content. However to reproduce more of it would distract from my intention to illustrate the analyst's receptive and expressive styles. When communication between analyst and patient verges on causing anguish, the structured discourse of either party may be broken. Then, thought and language, be they logical or lyrical, take on a dramatic expression that pushes the boundaries of the frame within which it develops. But, even outside of such tense situations, the analyst's interpretation often expresses itself dramatically, becoming as it does part of the internal or group drama that is staged within the session. J. Oriol Esteve and I (Folch & Esteve 1992) contrasted an understanding of the group as a multiple mind, with the notion of the individual mind as a space within which different facets of objects and of the self coexist. The analyst often spontaneously makes reference to the patient's inner group in his interpretation, as well as locating himself within the drama.

In conclusion I would say that to my mind, a good coexistence of the lyrical with the logical is necessary in the formulation of an interpretation. Such coexistence may ensure that the interpretative message is sufficiently rational, but unsaturated enough to leave room for the patient to be inspired by it. Such an interpretation can animate, or bring greater liveliness to the patient's subsequent communications. As I see it, this harmonious marriage of the logical and the lyrical can be expressed quite dramatically, as is illustrated in the vignette that references the horse or the goat. Such dramatic expression may see analyst and patient actualize, most vibrantly, the patient's unconscious drama. This actualization entails bringing into the realm of the present the unconscious that is intuited in the analyst's reverie, and expressed through his word.

Notes

1 Published in *Revista Catalana de Psicoanàlisi*, vol. XXII, nos 1–2, 2005.
2 Here Folch is contrasting the position of the poet with that of Paul's 2 Corinthians 4:13: "I believed, and so I spoke".

Bibliography

Ahumada, J. L. (1999) *Descubrimientos y refutaciones*. Madrid, APM, Biblioteca Nueva.
Bion, W. R. (1965) *Transformations*. London, Heinemann.

Bion, W. R. (1967) Notes on memory and desire. In *Melanie Klein Today*, vol. 2. London and New York, Routledge.

Bion, W. R. (1992) *Cogitations*. London, Karnac Books.

Bodner, G. (2000) Imaginación, regresión y creatividad. Lecture given at the Institut de Psicoanàlisi de Barcelona.

Bofill, P. and Folch, P. (1962) Problèmes cliniques et techniques du contre-transfert. *Rev. Franç. Psychanal*, vol. 27, special issue, pp. 31–129, 1963. XXIIIè Congrès des Psycanalystes de Langues Romàniques, Barcelona1962.

Britton, R. (1998) *Belief and Imagination*. London and New York, Routledge.

Carbó, F. (1990) *Joan Vinyoli: Escriptura poètica i construcció imaginària*. Inst. de Filologia Valenciana, Publicacions Abadia de Montserrat.

Coderch, J. (1995) *La interpretación en psicoanàlisis*. Barcelona, Herder.

Coromines, J. (1991) *Psicopatologia i desenvolupament arcaics*. Cap. 11. Barcelona, Espaxs.

Foix, J. V. (1936) *Sol i de dol*. Barcelona, L'Amic de les Arts, p. 26.

Folch, P. (1990) Procés psicoanalític i "procés literari". In *Psicoanàlisi i Literatura*. Barcelona, Fundació Caixa de Pensions..

Folch, P. (2001) *Descubrimientos y refutaciones: La lógica de la indagación psicoanalítica* [Discoveries and refutations: the logic of psychoanalytic enquiry]: Jorge L. Ahumada. Madrid, Asociación Psicoanalítica de Madrid, Biblioteca Nueva, 1999, 430 pp. Book Review of *Descubtimientos y refutaciones: La lógica de la indagación psicoanalítica*, by Jorge L. Ahumada. *Int. J. Psycho-Anal.*, vol. 82, no. 1, pp. 183–189.

Folch, P. and Esteve, J. O. (1992) Multiplicité de la psyché dans les groupes. *Revue psychothérapie. psychanalytique de groupe*, vol. 18.

Freixas, J. (1995) L'art poètica de Sigmund Freud. In *Debats a la cruïlla sobre el símbol*. Barcelona, PPU.

Freud, S. (1900) *The Interpretation of Dreams. The Standard Edition of the Complete Psychological Works of Sigmund Freud* 4: ix–627.

Freud, S. (1907) *Creative Writers and Day-Dreaming. The Standard Edition of the Complete Psychological Works of Sigmund Freud* 9: 141–154.

Hernàndez, V. (1992) Concepte psicoanalític de la funció simbòlica. Simbolisme "sensorial" i simbolisme "metafòric". *Rev. Catalana Psicoanàlisi*, vol. IX, 1–2.

Janés I Olivé, J. (1936) *Combat del somni*. Barcelona, Edicions de la Rosa dels Vents.

Kristeva, J. (1974) *La révolution du langage poétique*. Paris, Ed. du Seuil, p. 17.

Liberman, D. (1978) *Comunicación y Psicoanàlisis*. Buenos Aires, Alex Ed.

Ogden, T. H. (1999) "The music of what happens" in poetry and psychoanalysis. *Int. J. Psychoanal*, vol. 80, no. 5, p. 989.

Palau, I Fabre, J. (1997) *Quaderns de l'Alquimista*. Barcelona, Proa.

Riba, C. (1928) He cregut i és per això que he parlat. In *O.C.* III, p. 415ff. Barcelona, Edicions 62, 1986.

Riba, C. (1937) Un nu i uns ulls. In *O.C.* I, p. 144. Barcelona, Edicions 62, 1986.

Riba, C. (1953) Comentari a l'"Elegia III de Bierville". In *O.C.* III, Critica 2, pp. 251–252. Barcelona, Edicions 62, 1986.

Santaeulalia, J. N. (1989) *Qüestió de mots*. Barcelona, Edicions de la Magrana.

Tizón, J. L. (1978) *Introducción a la Epistemología de la Psicopatología y la Psiquiatría*. Barcelona, Ed. Ariel.

Torras, E. (1992) Gènesi del símbol en el procés terapèutic. *Rev. Catalana Psicoanàlisi*, vol. IX, 1–2.

Valéry, P. (1937) *Oeuvres*, I, pp. 1340ff. Paris, Gallimard.

Vinyoli, J. (1973) *Encara les paraules*. Barcelona, Ed. 62.

Vinyoli, J. (1975) *Ara que és tard*. Barcelona, Ed. 62.

Vinyoli, J. and Martí Pol, M. (1977) *Correspondència Barcelona. Roda de Ter*. Barcelona, Empúries.

Index

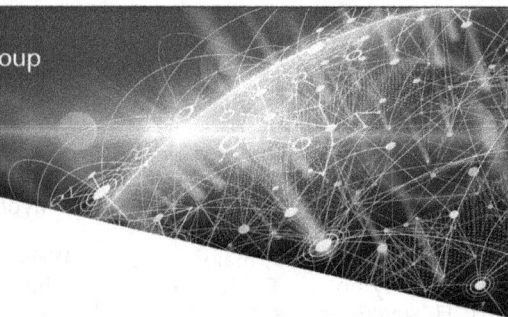

For Product Safety Concerns and Information please contact our EU
representative GPSR@taylorandfrancis.com
Taylor & Francis Verlag GmbH, Kaufingerstraße 24, 80331 München, Germany

www.ingramcontent.com/pod-product-compliance
Lightning Source LLC
Chambersburg PA
CBHW050609280326
41932CB00016B/2973